The Wheel of the Year with Animals as Guides

LADY WOLF

GREEN MAGIC

The Wheel of the Year with Animals as Guides
© 2022 by Lady Wolf.
All rights reserved. No part of this book may be used
or reproduced in any form without written permission
of the authors, except in the case of quotations in
articles and reviews.

Green Magic
Seed Factory
Aller
Langport
Somerset
TA10 0QN
England

www.greenmagicpublishing.com

Designed & typeset by Carrigboy, Wells, UK
www.carrigboy.co.uk

ISBN 978 1 8384185 9 5

GREEN MAGIC

As an eternal student of life, I would not be the person I am today if it was not for the many teachers who have blessed my life.

I dedicate this book to the Ancient Ones, my ancestors and the many, many teachers, mentors and elders who have sacrificed much in their lives and offered to let me sit at their feet and absorb their wisdom.

To my grandmother Ann, for teaching me to question everything.

To Mr Davies, my fifth grade teacher, for encouraging imagination.

To my sixth grade teacher, Ms Neilson, for prompting me to become a writer.

To my midwife Vickie, for knowledge and hands-on experience.

To my mother, for teaching me to see life through an artist's eyes.

To my father, for teaching me compassion and kindness for all.

To my lover and best friend Mason, for always believing in me.

To my children and granddaughter for endless lessons.

To the many Pagan, Wicca and witch mentors and teachers that I have had the pleasure to participate with in rituals, lectures and workshops; I thank you!

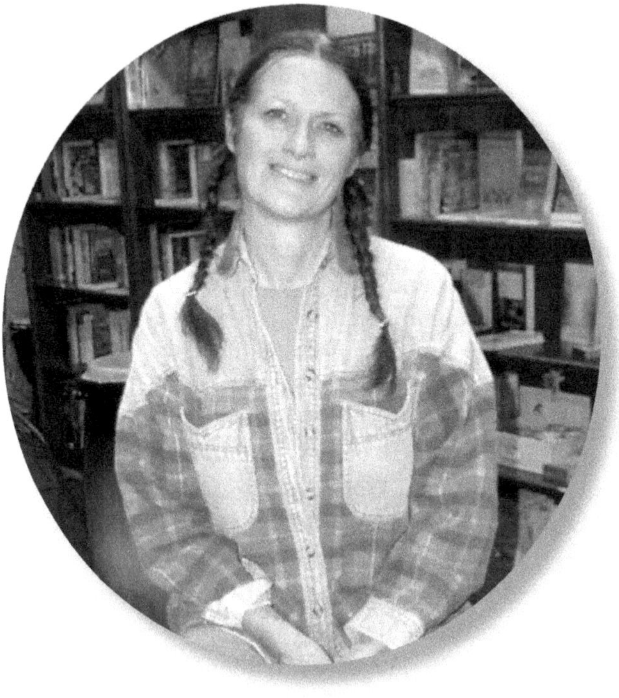

Tribute

In loving memory, I honor my teacher, mentor, guide, friend and matriarch, Michele Braun.

For eighteen years, Michele was patient, kind, empathetic, compassionate and loving with me as a 'not so easy to work with' student. Everything I do, she taught me. She would listen when I was struggling, she would hold me as I cried and she would challenge me every day to get up and be a better person today than I was yesterday.

One day a woman came up to me and asked me if I would help her connect with her animal totem. I informed her that Michele Braun is the best of the best and that she should seek her out to assist her with this as I was not quite trained enough to offer my assistance. She chuckled and replied "Michele told me to contact you, that you would be doing readings from here on out." Thus, my journey began with helping people connect to their spirit animals.

Michele passed away on Sunday, 29 August 2021, after a twenty-year battle with cancer. She was surrounded by her amazing family. What a legacy she has left. She was an angel on this earth and everyone who had the honor of knowing her was blessed. She will be greatly missed. She left a hole that will be impossible to fill.

Contents

Introduction	7
Chapter One: A Year and a Day Journey	9
Chapter Two: Making Contact with your Primary Spirit Animal (PSA)	21
Chapter Three: Honoring the Animals Reflected in Others	35
Chapter Four: The Wheel of the Year	45
Chapter Five: Signs and Symbols throughout the Year	54
Chapter Six: Seasonal Sabbat Animal Guides	63
Chapter Seven: Collection of Sabbat Ceremonies	90
Chapter Eight: Embracing Animism Day to Day	133
Chapter Nine: Animals you May Encounter; as you Turn the Wheel	145
Chapter Ten: Desert Sage Witchcraft – Practicing Animism Solitary and/or within a Pack	198
Bonus Chapter: An Anthology of Animal Mirrors	229

Introduction

At the beginning of the COVID-19 pandemic in February of 2020, I was gifted time as the Universe began a worldwide shift, awakening and a reckoning. In my efforts to find some peace and stay busy so as not to fall prey to fears and the unknown, I began to compile almost two decades of workshops, lectures, rituals and meditations into a book format.

Unbeknownst to me, and with great surprise, I was able to find a publisher that saw my vision and helped me bring to life *Animals as Gods*. Publishing my first book in the midst of a worldwide pandemic was truly the silver lining of my 2020 experience.

With the pandemic lasting much longer than anticipated, and with 'time' being ever prevalent, I have been bombarded with many more animals that wanted their voices, message and attributes to be shared.

When I completed *Animals as Gods* I was happily surprised to find that my little book of love and compassion for the animal kingdom was being embraced by many. So it is with great pleasure that I continue the journey into shapeshifting by once again honoring the animals as godlike messengers, mentors, guides and mirrors of how to live a more balanced and animistic life.

When we as humans can disconnect from the harmful belief that we are separate from the animal world and remember that we are also animals we can truly begin to relay compassion, empathy and allowance for others to move into a more primal and instinctual way of living and interacting with each individual.

This book is a tribute to the animal teachers who have come to me through my own personal journey into the practice of a year and a day commitment into studying witchcraft and educating myself on the many different Wiccan traditions; all in an effort to better implement a practice that fits my own unique and authentic flare.

THE WHEEL OF THE YEAR

As a practicing witch of twenty-six years, access to the Internet was not something that was readily available like it is today. In the beginning of my journey into the Craft books, animals and the seasons were my greatest sources of insight and education. Now we have a plethora of assets to help the 'new to witchcraft' to the 'seasoned witch' discover and appreciate ancient traditions and New Age modern day activities, allowing anyone to accomplish the Craft in their day to day lives.

Instead of the focus with a year and a day journey and the celebrating of the Celtic Wheel of the Year being centered on the old gods and the old ways of Paganism, this is a *shift* in perspective and a way to activate animism and see that the animals around us have been the ones turning the wheel all along.

When we take time each day, every day; to really be conscious of the world around us, we can begin to see that there are teachers everywhere. The animals on this great planet some call the Mama greatly outnumber us. In fact, humans only make up about 0.01% of all life on this great sphere. They are the number one predator on the planet. "Humanity has caused the loss of 83% of all wild animals and half of all plant life."

Something needs to change. We need to stop embracing the patriarchal mindset that the Earth belongs to us and that we, as humans, are the superior race, having dominion over the animals. This mindset is too detrimental to our survival on this planet. If we can survive the damage that we have done, we need to start now.

Shifting focus to animals as teachers, mentors, messengers and guides is a good place to begin. This mindset will create compassion and love for all animal life. But will it be enough? "Of all the mammals on Earth, 60% are livestock (that we as humans breed for our own gain), 36% are humans. If we honored "Animals as Gods," would we be eating them?

This book is a shift in perspective. A proposal to sit upon the Earth, the Great Mother Goddess and learn from her masters on how to live each day. The animals lead the way. We just need to follow.

CHAPTER ONE

A Year and a Day Journey

Witchcraft is on the rise! People from all over the world are actively engaged in a revival of the old ways and are now willing to admit it. The trend to come out of the broom closet is met with celebration! Since the 1990's, witchcraft as a practice and way of life has seen an increase.

In the American Religious Identification Survey, somewhere between 2001–2008, there has been an increase of Wiccans as well. This increase shows a big jump from 134,000 to 340,000. Paganism has seen a similar peak. In 2014, a religious landscape study was conducted by the Pew Research Center and, from that research, it is estimated that 0.3% of the entire US population now openly identifies as Wiccan or Pagan. That is big! That is worthy of celebrating. That number is also a reflection of those who openly participated in the survey. It is pretty safe to say that number has jumped tremendously with the arrival of social media platforms such as TikTok and Instagram; with common hashtags, such as #witchesofinstagram and #babywitches. These hash tags fuel the algorithms and allow for those practicing the craft to connect with other witches and build an online presence and community.

Whether or not witchcraft is becoming trendy or the cool thing to do, it is important for those new to the Craft, or #babywitches, to have some kind of basic direction so that they do not become overwhelmed. A basic 'year and a day' practice is time tested and proven to be very helpful to anyone who is venturing into the world of witchcraft, Paganism and/or deciding whether or not to embrace Wicca. It is vital to point out that ALL three are different and each one should be honored as a separate practice. It can be very offensive to just assume that all witches are Wiccans.

THE WHEEL OF THE YEAR

The year and a day time period is known as a bright line (an objective rule that resolves a legal issue in a straightforward, predictable manner) and can be found in a number of common law cases in both America and Europe.

The tradition of handfasting stems from Scotland and is a legal union, where a couple decide to live together for a year and a day. For some, this act is deemed legal by the common law of a year and a day commitment. At the end of the year and a day, the couple can decide to go their separate ways or pursue another year and a day commitment. It is quite beautiful and we are seeing an increase in handfastings being preferred over traditional wedding ceremonies.

Typically, a year and a day journey is focused on the many different and distinct Wiccan traditions, whereby an acting priest, priestess or coven mother suggests this time length of devotion and study into the particular tradition, before the seeker is initiated into the coven or tradition. For my students, a year and a day commitment is recommended before initiation is even considered. As a teacher, I want to ensure that anyone coming to me for training and insight is first and foremost committed and determined to learn as much as they can, using a self-paced training method that will help the individual grow on a spiritual level.

A year and a day journey builds commitment. It takes time, takes quite a bit of dedication. Author Timothy Roderick has written two books that take the individual on a day by day quest to dive in completely into a year and a day journey. While at times it may be redundant, we all know that repetition brings conviction. His first book is described as "ideal for solitary students, this intensive study course teaches the core content of Wiccan practice: the tides of time, the wonders of the seasons, the ways of herbs and magic, the mysticism of the old ones, and the inner disciplines of seers and sages." His *Year and a Day* books consist of daily lessons, Wiccan theology and much, much more. It is important that those curious souls who desire to make this kind of commitment have options!

When diving into the realm of witchcraft and Wicca it is very easy to become discouraged as one must remember there are NO sacred set texts that tell the individual what to believe, how to live and how to implement one's practice into one's day to day life. To dive in, one must be prepared to be exposed to whatever the individual author's concept and experience is, then the reader must be able to be self-motivated and develop their own unique practice, especially if they are seeking a solitary path.

In Wicca, there are literally hundreds of different traditions. While both Wicca and witchcraft are anchored into Paganism, there are some distinctions. For example, in a Wiccan tradition, there are quite often rules, sacred agreements and codes of ethics determined and implemented by the founders or leaders of that particular tradition. Some examples of those traditions, just to name but a few of the most common ones, are Gardnerian, Alexandrian, Dianic, eclectic, Hermetic and Seax Wicca. For each of these traditions, there are distinctions in how the Craft within is practiced, what to wear, how to set up one's altar, who can join, etc…

As a triple ordained high priestess I represent three distinct branches or traditions of Wicca, the first being a combination of Alexandrian/Hermetic, the second being very eclectic and the third ordination coming from the foremother of the actual Wiccan tradition, Zsuzsuanna Budapest, herself Dianic. While a representative and acting high priestess, it is my responsibility to showcase these lineages and allow for others to circle with me and experience these traditions. I am also a genetic witch, meaning that in my ancestry line I have actual witches who I honor by doing the work that I do in both a solitary and public setting.

A public website that is quite helpful, *www.wiccaliving.com* has this to say: "Wicca is and has always been a dynamic religion, changing and evolving over time as more and more people are drawn to learn, interpret and integrate its core tenets into their own experiences. While there are many traditionalists adhering as closely as they can to the 'original' form of the Craft developed by Gerald Gardner, the explosion of interest in Wicca over the past several decades has led to new forms and pathways that continue to lead in new directions.

THE WHEEL OF THE YEAR

Indeed, the possibilities might even seem overwhelming to newcomers to the Craft, but all you need to do is remain open while exploring your options. Listen to your intuition and follow where your heart leads you. As long as you do so, there are no wrong turns.

This is where a year and a day journey comes into play in assisting one in finding out and feeling what is out there for you if you want to be practitioner of the Craft or are already one. In a world where the only thing constant is change, and society is changing as we all learn to adapt and grow, being an eternal student should be a priority. There are literally hundreds of different branches of Wiccan traditions, why not research as many of them as possible before claiming one as your one and only?

After all, the reason eclectic witchcraft and solitary witches are increasing in number is because there is not the stigma and old dogma that "this way is the only way." For years, I offered a Dianic coven. It was 'invite only' and with the stipulation that each new potential member complete a year and a day study that, as priestess, I created. If, at the end of the year and a day, the student decided that the Dianic tradition was not a good fit for them, then they went on with their way or, together, we explored different traditions. As priestess, I am dedicated to education, not proselyting. I am not doing this work to convert and acquire more students. For me, the work of serving my community as a priestess is just that; a work in service. I simply hold open a door and become a gateway for students to see that there is so much to learn and so many different ways to implement one's teachings and practice them in one's day to day life. One question I always ask my students is: "why limit yourself?"

The year and a day study that is recommended to my students and those who come to me seeking a direction of where to begin making a journey into the Craft and practice of witchcraft features a new lesson each week. The student is asked to spend at least 10–30 minutes per day on that particular lesson of the week before moving onto the next week's lesson. This gives the student incentive to create a day to day devotion dedicated to their individual learning and growth.

In my active solitary life as a witch, I have personally completed a year and a day journey six times. Not an easy task, because life gets in the way. However, there were times where I shifted my focus on doing my year and a day studies to help me disconnect from what was happening in my life.

Week 1: History of witchcraft
(Each day research the history, record your findings, document things that stand out to you. At the end of the week please compile your findings in a one page essay)

Week 2: Wicca as a Nature religion
(Each day write something new that confirms your research of Wicca being a Nature religion. At the end of the week please write your findings in a one page essay)

Week 3: The Wiccan Rede – long version
(Recite, write and memorize)

Week 4: The Mother Goddess
(Research and spend time with the different versions on the Mother Goddess in different pantheons and cultures)

Week 5: What is a deity?
(Get to know what a deity is, make a list. Which ones call to you?)

Week 6: What does happiness mean to you? How can you achieve it? How can you live it?

Week 7: The Goddess?
(Who is she? What is she? How many are there? Which goddesses speak to you?)

Week 8: Developing memorization skills
(Seek out techniques to help you memorize)

Week 9: The Charge of the Goddess
(Recite, write and memorize)

Week 10: Write your own charge

Week 11: Organizational skills
(Organize your sacred space, organize your home, de-clutter, clear out those things that no longer serve you)

Week 12: Dianic witchcraft
(What is it? Who founded it? How can you embrace it? Is this path for you?)

Week 13: Egyptian witchcraft
(What is it? Who founded it? How can you embrace it? Is this path for you?)

Week 14: Triple Goddess
(Explain, name and write a one page essay on your findings)

Week 15: Meditation
(What types are there? Which ones do you prefer?)

Week 16: Cone of power
(What is it? How is it achieved? Spend time raising a cone of power)

Week 17: Ethics of magic
(Write them down, memorize them, live them!)

Week 18: Types of magic
(Research)

Week 19: Law of Attraction
(Research, read, and watch *The Secret*)

Week 20: Altar tools and altar layout
(Create an altar dedicated to your path of Wiccan discovery)

Week 21: The pentagram
(Research and draw)

Week 22: The elements
(Why do we work with them?)

Week 23: Air
(Spend time with air, what are its qualities?)

Week 24: Fire
(Spend time with fire, what are its qualities?)

Week 25: Water
(Spend time with water, what are its qualities?)

Week 26: Earth
(Spend time with earth, what are its qualities?)

Week 27: Spirit
(spend time with your own definition of spirit, how do you contact and connect with spirit?)

Week 28: Circle casting
(Read different circle castings, find one that resonates with you)

Week 29: Create and write your own circle casting
(Memorize)

Week 30: Perform casting with high priestess

Week 31: Spells
(What are they? How do they work?)

Week 32: Write your own spell

Week 33: Wheel of the Year

Week 34: Samhain
(History, how to celebrate, write down your own ritual – do this for all the sabbats)

Week 35: Yule

Week 36: Imbolc

Week 37: Ostara

Week 38: Beltane

Week 39: Litha

Week 40: Lughnasadah

Week 41: Mabon

Week 42: Green witchery
(What is it?)

Week 43: Create a witch's medicine cabinet

Week 44: Design a medicine wheel garden
(Get to know the herbs you will be planting, what are their healing properties)

Week 45: Craft your own herbal tonics
(Hands on at high priestesses house)

Week 46: Lunar phases
(Understand, draw, memorize)

Week 47: Design a lunar garden
(What plants go in a lunar garden? How to harvest by the moon phases)

Week 48: Invoking the Goddess
(Research invoking, pick a goddess to call)

Week 49: Write your invocation and invoke
(Understand the difference between evoking and invoking before proceeding)

Week 50: Facing your shadow self
(What are your fears, what are your insecurities? Dig deep, learn to embrace your dark side as much as your light side)

Week 51: Review your year
(What are the highlights, how have you embraced this path, is Wicca for you?)

Week 52: Are you ready to identify as witch?
(Contemplate, review and decide)

Is a year and a day an absolute, vital journey that one MUST take in order to successfully practice witchcraft? NO! But it does help tremendously! So many 'new to the craft' witches are longing for direction and a way to describe their individual practice to not only others but to themselves. A year and a day helps any witch to anchor into what resonates truth and not what doesn't.

So, while I have provided a very basic and general inquiry of a year and a day journey into what one's witchcraft practice could look like, my focus with this book is to help you the reader gain an understanding and relationship with the animals that offer us mere humans insight and direction on a day to day basis. So, below you will find an animistic approach to a year and a day journey.

A YEAR AND A DAY WITH ANIMALS LEADING THE WAY

Please spend 10–30 minutes per day researching each weekly assignment. Fill at least one page in your journal or book of shadows for each day of researching.

Week One: What is animism?
Week Two: What is the history of animal totem work?
Week Three: What is the difference between animal totems and spirit animals?
Week Four: What is shapeshifting?
Week Five: What is animistic witchcraft?

Week Six: Spend a week with birds. What is the life cycle of birds? How does a bird's life cycle mirror your own cycle or phases of life?
Week Seven: Work with the element of air, direction of east, and gain an understanding of the role air currents play in the flight patterns of birds.
Week Eight: Dedicate a week to one particular bird, create an altar of dedication for that particular bird and honor any similarities you may share.
Week Nine: Embody the essence of bird. In what areas of your life can you exercise a new perspective or a bird's eye view? Are there situations in your life that you need to fly away from or fly towards? In which ways can you welcome the phases of birds into your day to day life?
Week Ten: Create a bird feeder or aviary sanctuary in your yard and spend time each day observing birds in your area, how they act, what they look like and make note of all the different species of birds.
Week Eleven: What is mirror work?
Week Twelve: How are animals a mirror?
Week Thirteen: Research animals as messengers
Week Fourteen: Research the connection that animals have with ancient gods & goddesses.
Week Fifteen: What is a witch's familiar?
Week Sixteen: Think back on your life. What animals have you had or wanted? Why? What impact did they make on your life?
Week Seventeen: If you could be any animal, what would it be, and why?
Week Eighteen: If you have an animal in your home, spend time each day mirroring its movements. Embody physically the way your animal moves. If you do not have an animal, then pick one and study it online via *Youtube* or another resource. Watch that animal and physically copy its movement.
Week Nineteen: Dive into the different religions that practice animism.
Week Twenty: What are the hunter-gatherer cultures and why do they play a role in today's search for and new resurgence of animism?
Week Twenty-One: Spend some time honoring the current season you are in. What are some common things about this season? What animals are associated with this season and why?
Week Twenty-Two: Create a seasonal celebration that is dedicated to one animal that is associated with this current season you are experiencing.
Week Twenty-Three: Research at least three reptiles that live in your area. What are their characteristics? What do you like about them and what do you not like about them?

THE WHEEL OF THE YEAR

Week Twenty-Four: Dedicate a week to one particular reptile, create an altar of dedication for that particular reptile and honor any similarities you may share.

Week Twenty-Five: Embody the essence of reptile. In which areas of your life are you in need of shedding? Maybe you need to harness the power of the Sun in order to grow and expand? Are their situations in your life which mirror to you the need to let old patterns die in order to move forward?

Week Twenty-Six: Select at least one reptile and research its different life phases. Do you share any similarities with each phase?

Week Twenty-Seven: Are there any ancient gods or goddesses associated with reptiles? For example, what do the Medusa's snakes on her head really symbolize? Spend time researching the different deities associated with animals and find one that resonates with you.

Week Twenty-Eight: Create a focal altar dedicated to the deity you chose the week prior. How can you relate to this deity?

Week Twenty-Nine: Research one particular reptile of your choice and study its physical structure. In what ways do you wear armor? What does it protect you from? If your armor is your scales, what condition are they in? Is it time to let things go? Or time to revamp your scaled protection?

Week Thirty: Establish a relationship with dragons in your energetic realm. Research dragons, maybe draw or paint a dragon. What roles did dragons play in the lives of your ancestors? What role can dragons play in your current realm?

Week Thirty-One: Work with the element of fire, direction of south. Gain an understanding of how fire, heat and sunlight are vital for a reptile's survival. How are they vital for yours?

Week Thirty-Two: Dive into water animals. Do you have any natural water sources nearby? If so, what animals live within? Select at least three to research. If you do not have water nearby, then simply select three water animals that you feel an affection towards.

Week Thirty-Three: Select at least one water animal to research, create an altar of dedication to it and observe any similarities you may have with that water animal.

Week Thirty-Four: What is your personal relationship with water? How do you connect with water, rely upon it and how do you use water for transformation and healing?

Week Thirty-Five: Work with the element of water, spend physical time in water, honor the direction of the west. How does west relate to the element of water?

Week Thirty-Six: How can you use water animals as mirrors? Are there areas in your life that you need to float upon instead of act? Are there waves that are more intense than others? How can you maneuver through these aspects as water?

Week Thirty-Seven: How do ocean animals ride the wave currents? Research the different layers of the Ocean and what animals live in each layer. Is there a layer that you would anchor into as home?

Week Thirty-Eight: Research the food chain in your nearby water source (ocean, river, lake). Which animal predator or prey do you relate to the most and why?

Week Thirty-Nine: If you could be any animal in the ocean, what would it be? Why? Create a vision board that embodies attributes of this animal that you can mirror in your own life.

Week Forty: Research the desert as a metaphor for life. Can you see your own life as having similarities with the desert?

Week Forty-One: What does your inner desert (or ego/shadow) realm currently look like? In what ways are you parched and thirsting for more?

Week Forty-Two: What mammals live in your area? Research your local wildlife and select three that you can spend time developing a relationship with. How have humans imposed upon their natural way of life?

Week Forty-Three: Get to know the insects in your area. Take time to learn about them, observe them and if there are any that you are uneasy about and spend extra time with those and mend that disconnect.

Week Forty-Four: Select one local animal and create a devotional altar to it. Do you share any similarities with this animal? What attributes can you mirror within your own life?

Week Forty-Five: Move through the 'primary animal spirit activation meditation' (see p.25) within this book and write down which animal came through as your primary animal mirror? What similarities do you have? How did you feel making contact? What was your meditation like?

Week Forty-Six: How do you already embody your primary animal spirit? Have you worked with this animal before? Have you worked with the shared attributes within yourself before?

Week Forty-Seven: How are you predator? How are you prey? Do these attributes have anything to do with your ego? Can you honor both and embrace balance within? Can you honor the predator and prey aspects in those you come into contact with or live with?

Week Forty-Eight: The zoo you live with ... Invite your family to participate in the primary animal spirit activation meditation. Start honoring each other as individual animals free from expectations and stipulations. After all, a bear would never demand a blue jay be anything other than a blue jay. Make a family altar that showcases each individual animal that you connected with.

Week Forty-Nine: Start to be more observant. Each day we are blessed with animals as messengers, teachers, mentors and guides. Spend at least five to ten minutes outside, open to receive. Journal and research whatever animal appears. Or pick one at random and research it. Be sure to apply the attributes of each animal as a mirror. Start living more consciously aware of the role animals play.

Week Fifty: See yourself as an animal. What are your basic survival needs? What food sustains you and what food depletes you? What element is home to you and what element do you dislike? Start trusting your gut more and stop dismissing it! When you second-guess your animal instincts, you step into ego brain and can cause unnecessary havoc to occur within your life.

Week Fifty-One: Nature is the greatest teacher. Spend more time outdoors, anchor into her healing allies and step into a more animistic conscious way of living. After all, animism isn't just about seeing animals as Divine but seeing all as Divine. Create an outdoor sanctuary for yourself. Gift yourself time outdoors in Nature.

Week Fifty-Two: Imagination is your greatest tool. Start taking time each day to meditate. You can call upon any animal that you wish to activate its desired attributes simply by moving into a meditative connection practice. For example, if you need a birds' eye view in your subconscious, see yourself as a bird flying above the issue you are facing and looking at it from a different angle. Each day this week, spend time connecting with a different animal and honor the attributes that you share by applying them to your day to day.

Once you have selected which year and a day journey you are wanting to begin with, then you are ready to dive deeper into this journey of activating connection with animals to assist you.

Let this chapter be an anchor that you refer back to weekly when you are ready for your next assignment.

But for now, let's find that mirror! What animal is a reflection of you as you are right now? What animal will serve as your primary spirit animal on your quest through this next year and a day?

CHAPTER TWO

Making Contact with your Primary Spirit Animal

Have you ever found yourself mind-numbingly scrolling on Facebook or the Internet and stumbled upon a personality quiz like "discover your spirit animal?" Or have you ever been interviewed for a job and the one conducting the interview asked you, "if you were an animal, which would you be, and why?" There are roughly 102,000,000 different sites, links and apps devoted to helping one discover their animal personality, inner animal, spirit animal, totem animal, and so on.

In 1995, a non-fiction book was published, titled *The Animal in You*, by author Roy Feinson, features a personality test that will lump you into one of 45 possible personality types. With these animal personalities broken down into carnivores, herbivores, birds, reptiles, rodents and insectivores. A personality test by definition is a "method of assessing human personality constructs. Most personality assessment instruments are in fact introspective self-report questionnaires." The very first personality assessment measures were actually developed in the 1920's and were "intended to ease the process of personnel selection, particularly in the armed forces."

The question is: are they even effective? Scientific American posted an article in response to personality testing back in 2018, stating "in a way, it's disappointing. It just means that a personality test can only tell you what you tell it." You won't learn anything that you didn't already know about yourself, and its accuracy comes entirely from how honest and self-reflective you were with your answers.

THE WHEEL OF THE YEAR

To help me really see this in action, I sent out an inquiry while percolating and brewing this book into fruition and asked all those who responded to participate in one of many "find your spirit animal" personality quizzes online or via an app. Then I offered them a response questionnaire with the following questions:

1. Did you find the quiz helpful?
2. Do you see any similarities with yourself and the animal you were linked with?
3. Did you find that the questions really spotlighted your individual characteristics?
4. Or did you find the questions easy to manipulate and sway in the direction of what animal you really desired to be matched with?
5. Do you think these types of quiz are really effective in helping one to honor animals as mirrors?

The problem with these type of quizzes is that they are not backed by any scientific evidence. They are typically a fun way to pass the time, unless you end up being matched with an animal that you just despise. In which case, you can just keep taking the quiz over and over until you achieve the desired result.

While I do think that posing the question "if you were an animal what would you be?" can be insightful into understanding a potential client or employee, it too is a pretty broad question that is really based upon how the person chooses to respond.

In my line of work as a shapeshifting priestess, I have had the opportunity to help connect over a thousand clients to their primary animal messenger, mirror or guide. While oftentimes I get asked if I look around a room and tell people what their animal messenger, mirror or guide is, based on their outward appearance, I always answer with an honest "no." It is not my place to decide for anyone else what their primary or current animal messenger, mirror or guide is. That is a very intimate connection and there should be some time and energy invested into establishing that contact with a particular animal.

What I do like is the commonality shared amongst almost all of the animal personality quizzes, and that is; all humans have shared attributes and characteristics with animals and they behave similarly to the animals they are matched with.

Just for fun, you can visit the *animalinyou.com* website and take their quiz and answer the questions from above. While it is fascinating to me that over 20 million people have taken their animal personality quiz, I wonder what those 20 million participants did with the information provided. How did they implement the animal given into their lives?

What I learned from the study I performed with clients was that, yes, each individual could in one way relate to the animal they received as a result from the quiz, but they also all agreed that the answers were too easy to manipulate and one could very easily dictate the result. I believe that if we really disconnect from the societal narrative that humans are superior to animals and remember that we ARE animals, then we can find similarities with any animal we match with, in any of the hundreds of thousands of quizzes floating around the web.

With shapeshifting however, we do more than just identify with one animal's attributes; we actually take techniques, like ones mentioned in my first book, and we implement them through ritual and ceremony to create a space within our energetic field where we can morph and blend our current reality with the animal we have chosen. This is something that anyone can do. It really is all about the intention and the energy you invest into establishing this link between human and animal.

So, with the online quizzes, the intention seems to be something fun. Do I think they are an actual guide to what one's spirit animal or personal totem is? NO! I think that they are good sneak peek into the possibilities of what animal magic has the potential to create in one's life and community.

To begin to really dive into the power of utilizing shapeshifting to enhance relationships, it helps to understand where you vibe right now. What animal essence are you mirroring out into the world? How can you step into this animal essence and really begin to shift things in your life?

HOW THE EXERCISE WORKS

First, we go into a meditative space and mindset which disconnects us from ego and the urge to manipulate.

Second, we go through a cave which is meant to clear any childbirth trauma and prepare you for this powerful connection of seeing an animal as a mirror image of who you are right now in this moment.

Third, the animal chooses you, not the other way around. As a hypnotherapist, I have found that every person is capable of being hypnotized because one's individual choice to relax and follow the prompts given in meditation is completely in their control. We all possess the ability to quiet our mind and enter a relaxed state where our subconscious becomes a sponge soaking up the prompts offered by the one doing the meditation. In this state, where our subconscious and conscious brain are aligned, it is difficult to manipulate a meditation, although not impossible. I have had many clients attempt to force the outcome of a guided meditation and the results were nothing to really brag about or write home about because they chose to not submit to the process, they let ego brain take control.

Fourth, what you do with the animal that comes through in your meditation is completely up to you as it is your connection and mirror to see, honor and expand upon.

Are you ready?

I invite you to create a physical location that will be free from interruption. Maybe you would like to light a candle and dim the lights creating a more ritual or ceremonial experience. The key really is to give yourself permission to relax and be open to guided prompts. Some people are more visual and can see clearly what is being described as if they were watching a movie on a screen, while others are more kinesthetic and can feel what is being described but not seen. Again, as an individual, your way of moving through meditation is completely up to you. Also, the animal that comes through in meditation is as unique as you are and may surprise you, may even disappoint you. But it is important to honor and allow yourself time to digest and reflect.

While it is simple to take a quiz online; moving energetically towards establishing a connection with your primary animal messenger, mirror or guide through meditation is a more effective way of seeing into your subconscious, free from ego and the judgments that you place upon yourself.

Before we begin with the meditation, please know that you can access a recording of this particular meditation via my Youtube channel link found at the back of this book. If you are taking this journey into shapeshifting with a partner, you can take turns reading the meditation to each other. This act of leading each other through this activation will be an excellent way of kick-starting your intent to enhance your relationship with shapeshifting animism. Think of this vital step of activating connection with your current animal essence as establishing a baseline like a medical professional would before offering treatment.

ENTER THE MEADOW OF CONNECTION MEDITATION

Begin by sitting or lying down in a comfortable position and focus on your breath.

Take intentional time to inhale nice and slowly and exhale nice and slowly. Feel your breath move through your body as your chest rises with each exhale and your shoulders relax with each exhale.

Very gently, allow your eyes to close and, while you breathe, enjoy how good it feels to just let your eyes rest as you consciously clear your mind of any wandering thoughts with each inhale and each exhale. Breathing in to the count of four and exhaling out to the count of four.

Breathe in…2…3…4… and breathe out…2…3…4…

(repeat five times)

Allow yourself to create your own rhythm of breath that is nice and slow as you take inventory of your physical body. Breathe in to the top of your head and releasing any tension there, in your forehead, your eyes, your mouth and your jaw. Allow your jaw to open ever so slightly as you consciously release any tension. Feel this flow of relaxation drift down your neck, to your shoulders all the way down to your forearms and fingertips. Feel as your arms become heavy. This heavy calm relaxation moves through your chest, your stomach, down to your hips. … Moving down your thighs, calves, all the way down to your toes. In this position of sitting or lying down, your entire physical body is relaxed.

In this state of calm, you are ready to move into your mind's eye where you visualize yourself sitting in your favorite spot in Nature. This can be a location you have visited many times or a place you have always wanted to go. Here, in this place in Nature, you are safe, relaxed and aware of all that surrounds you, the grass beneath you, the rocks, the trees, the sky above. It is here in this place that your conscious mind will stay to rest, while we journey inward with your subconscious.

Taking another slow breath in…2…3…4… and out…2…3…4…

(repeat five times)

You are now in a space of deep, deep relaxation and in your mind's eye you can see before you a pathway that leads further into the forest. There is a strong urge to follow this path as it winds through the thick trees. So, you move step by step, feeling each foot sink into the spongy ground of the forest. As the trees thicken on both sides of the path, you see that the pathway is not long and that it leads to a large cave entrance. Standing before this large cave, you feel an even stronger pull to enter the dark of the cave. Unsure but calm, you enter the cave, moving into the darkness. Feeling tiny rocks beneath you and the cave walls inching closer to you as you move deeper and deeper into the cave. You can extend both your arms out and touch the sides of the cave. When you reach above, you feel the smooth and somewhat cold dampness of the stone as this cave gently surrounds you. It is common to feel a little bit of discomfort and tightness in the cave but the urge to continue is so strong that you allow your senses to take over, utilizing touch to help you maneuver in the darkness, moving over boulders and tight spaces, you are just about to be taken over by frustration when there appears to be a light before you. Maybe this cave is not a cave. As you move forward with more vigor, you begin to see that this cave was really a tunnel. Light of day is shining through and with the last few steps you can see clearly every stone before you. As you take your last step out of the tunnel, you see before you more forest.

(pause)

You can feel the heat from the Sun above you, warming your face. You feel the soft and gentle breeze as it lightly caresses your skin. Here before you is another path. This one paved with dirt and pine needles. It is spongy and,

MAKING CONTACT WITH YOUR PRIMARY SPIRIT ANIMAL

as you step upon it, again you follow that urge; that pull to keep going – so you do. You follow the path as it winds through the forest, you feel the trees becoming thicker, you smell the forest air clean and invigorating. You may even hear animals moving in the forest as you make your way along this winding path through the trees. When you come to the end of the path, you see before you a meadow filled with wildflowers. You watch as the gentle breeze nods the flowers back and forth, giving the appearance that they are dancing. The meadow is so calm that you decide to sit down at the entrance and just gaze out onto it.

(pause)

On the far side of the meadow, you see the forest continues and the trees look much thicker on that side. Gazing out at the far side of the meadow, you begin to see a shadow moving through the trees. You may even hear animal noises coming from that side of the meadow. Your heart rate begins to increase as you anxiously anticipate the shadow to reveal itself. Just wait. Just watch as an animal steps out from the shadows and makes its way to the center of the meadow.

(pause)

Give yourself permission to be open and see the animal that has reached the center of the meadow. Observe how it moves, what color is it? What size is it? Here, in the center of the meadow, the animal waits, waits for you to join it. Knowing you are safe and the animal waiting for you has chosen you as a mirror, you slowly begin to move from where you were sitting and you make your way to the center of the meadow where the animal is waiting and watching you with the same curiosity you showed it.

(pause)

Here in the center of the meadow, with the animal before you, honor connection through closer observation. Really see in detail the animal and, when you are ready, reach out and touch it.

Make physical contact. Feel the animal against your skin, what does it feel like? What are you feeling emotionally as you make physical contact with your animal messenger, guide and mirror?

(pause)

Now that you have seen and felt your animal, listen to its call. How does it speak to you? Does it have a name? Does it have a specific message for you? When you look into its eyes, what do they convey? Here in the center of the meadow, just you and your animal, I want you to just be. Mimic each other's movements. With connection established, you are ready to leave the meadow. This time you are not alone as your animal joins you. Together you both move onto the path as it winds back through the forest and thick trees. Together, you both enter the cave knowing now that it is just a tunnel.

Where before there was unease, now you feel at peace as your animal journeys with you into the tunnel, offering companionship and security, as if a piece of you has been reclaimed and you feel more whole than you have in a very long time. Together you both move through the tight spaces, over the boulders and into the dark, until the tunnel opens up and daylight once again fills the entrance.

(pause)

Together, you both move back along the path where it leads to that space in Nature, where you left your conscious mind to rest. You sit back down upon the forest floor and, bringing your awareness back to your breath, you feel your animal breathing beside you in unison. Together, you both breathe back into your physical body, your subconscious joining with your conscious mind as your breath begins to awaken you. You slowly begin to wiggle your fingers and toes as you breathe back into this hear and this now. With each breath, you slowly begin to awaken more and more.

Feeling a sense of peace, calm and assurance that you have made a very powerful connection which has brought you into a state of wholeness.

JOURNAL PROMPT

What animal appeared in the meadow? How did you feel when you made contact? Is this an animal you were expecting?

As a shapeshifting priestess, this meditation is one of my favorites to offer to clients and students. To see the look on each individual's face as they begin to open their eyes is really transformational. For me, as I am leading the meditation, the room begins to fill up rather quickly with a variety of mixed energies as each individual's animal begins to appear. There is a distinct change.

This is a meditation that can be done daily when wanting to tap into animals as messengers on a daily basis, but for the intent of this book; this meditation is our baseline. With this connection as a primary one, being one that takes up time and focus, it is not uncommon to have the same animal appear as primary for many, many years. So, invest some time in honoring this connection before diving into the meditation again.

The importance of seeing this connection as primary will be a state of devotion. Not only is this animal an extension of your already existent energy but it can be your greatest messenger, teacher, mentor and guide, as you maneuver and take anchor in new relationships. While it is a beautiful thought there, not everyone you interact with will be open to taking this journey with you and participating in the meditation; we are all individuals and we must honor people to journey at their own pace and comfort.

So really, how you engage with this connection will be of utmost importance when understanding why you engage with others the way you do. For example, my primary animal mirror has been a wolf for the past ten years. This is not an animal I felt comfortable with. I was actually scared of it when it first came through but, with time, I have learned to see that I do indeed behave as a wolf does when interacting with others. I tend to sniff out the parameters with investigation before going into an unknown space. I tend to be cautious when meeting new people and really tap into my guttural physical and innate responses to let me know if I should pursue an interaction or flee.

But now I am getting ahead of myself! Let's shift back. Now that you have established this connection with your primary animal mirror, what do you do next? Let's start with the steps discussed in my first book, *Animals as Gods*, and begin with observation. What animal appeared to you? Do you have a means to observe this animal in person, probably not! However, in this day and age of modern technology, you can literally Google any animal and hundreds of videos and articles will appear. So, begin there, I often tell my clients that Youtube is my chosen tool for observation. Take a few days or weeks to really see how your animal behaves in a somewhat natural habitat. How is it predator and how is it prey?

Next, activate visualization by writing down any similarities you may have. For example, I found through this step that I have a tendency to literally show teeth when I am feeling threatened by another I am engaging with. I never realized I did this until I started to really pay attention. Visually I can see quite a few similarities in how I behave in my community, when compared to how a wolf behaves in its pack. So, make a list.

The third step is to meditate, often! Sit in a quiet space whenever you can and intentionally invite your animal to join you in this space and feel, see and allow the animal to give you messages and insight as to why this animal is your mirror and how you mirror it to the outside world.

The fourth step is mirror through movement work. In my first book, each animal chapter had a yoga pose to physically activate this mirroring movement exercise. For the sake of this book, I want you activate what you have observed and literally move your body in a mimicking way. As a wolf, part of my shapeshifting rituals consist of wolf movement. Digging my claws into the ground, growling, howling, moving with precision and basically doing whatever my son's dog Gus does, as he is very large and the closest thing I have to a wolf in my home.

The last step is really bringing all the steps together through study. Taking time to research is all part of developing a connection with your animal that is more meaningful. After all, this animal is not separate from you – it is an extension of your primal, raw energetic state that is a part of who you are. That inner wildness is this animal, right here, right now. So get to know it. What characteristics do you both share? How do you both interact with others? Where are you on the food chain?

As wolf, I am predator, but like all creatures; I am also prey. Understanding that both aspects have to be embraced in order for there to be wholeness is vital. There are some people that I clash with monumentally, especially within the structures of my community. For example, my daughter's main animal is quite literally the king of the jungle – the lion. She and I do things very differently and with her characteristics being more cat-like, this wolf tends to become easily annoyed and show teeth which results in her showing even larger teeth. My lover of twenty years is a bear (which we will go into more detail of later on), he appears to move at a much slower pace than this wolf. In actuality, I lack the patience that he possesses. So, while I think he is dragging his feet, I tend to nip at his heels, which always causes the big bear in him to end up growling if I don't take the hints to back off.

How we embrace ourselves as connected with our primary animal opens up so many doors of insight into every relationship we form because it creates a shift in our thought process. We begin to start being more allowing of others to be themselves because we don't see them as humans, we see them as animals. Would you ever go into the forest and demand that a deer behave like a raven? No! But as humans, we project and demand expectations followed by stipulations onto other humans if they behave in ways that we choose to be offended by. The intent with this book is to start to see the wild in each other, for we are ALL animals. When we can begin to embrace certain attributes, quirks or characteristics as being similar with animals, we begin to soften how we react towards those we have relations and interactions with.

Through shapeshifting, we can begin to call upon certain animal attributes in an effort to embody them in our everyday life. We live in a world where unfortunately the mass population still believes that humans are superior to the animals. That we possess dominion over the animals. That we are the boss! Where referring to another human as an animal or sharing animal characteristics is "dehumanizing, as humans are moral, civil and smart: animals are not. Humans sit one step above animals. To call someone an animal is therefore to demote them to a lower rung of existence, a more primitive state of being where they lack human virtues." If that quote upset you like it did me then this is the book for you.

I invite you to journey with me as together we embark upon a new perspective of shapeshifting, working with different animals as mirrors, embracing them through myth and legends as they once were seen as gods, and activate those connections through rituals and ceremonies to create peace and insight in to how we interact with ourselves and with others.

It's time to reclaim our connection with each other as animals. It's time to allow animal essences to flow through us so that we can soften our egos and really create a space of love and allowance.

In the book, *The Wisdom of Wolves*, author Elli H. Radinger says, "If it's possible in Nature for different species to live together for their own advantage and be friends, why is it so hard for us humans to come to terms even with representatives of our own species with different origins or skin color?" We are quite literally engaged in a battle with our own species on an almost daily basis. Social media has allowed us a platform that encourages predator and prey-like attacks. Even the slightest disagreement can become the dissolution of a lifelong friendship! Families are turning on each other and compassion seems to be almost extinct. I believe the remedy to this hate can be found in Nature. As Nature is the ultimate healer and recycler. I believe that when we start seeing each other as vibrations of animal essences, we will begin to practice more appreciation and begin to allow each other as animals a space to show up as they are. When we can accept that each day we are going to be bit different then the day before, we are stepping into a conscious way of life that is not ruled by gender roles, relationship obligations, stipulations or expectations. We are discovering Nature within not just ourselves, but those around us.

https://theconversation.com/why-its-so-offensive-when-we-call-people-animals-76295

THE WITCH'S FAMILIAR

By definition, a familiar is "well known from long or close association, often encountered or experienced, having good knowledge of, close friendship, intimate." When used as a noun in the dictionary, they give this example: 'A demon supposedly attending and obeying a witch, often said to assume the form of an animal." In encyclopedias, they list familiar as: "In Western demonology, small animal or imp kept as a witch's attendant, given to her by the Devil or inherited from another witch. The familiar was a low-ranking demon that assumed any animal shape, such as a toad, dog, insect, or black cat. Sometimes the familiar was described as grotesque."

Big sigh The stereotypes and superstitions are still ever prevalent! Let's break it down shall we? We know that the root word of *witch* is *wit* meaning *wise*. When we combine that with a familiar, we can fairly say that a witch's familiar is an animal or something the witch is close to that is used as a companion to assist in a wise manner. Ok, that is my definition. For the sake of this book, and the intent behind it, my definition will work. If you don't like it, then come up with your own. But for hell's sake, let's stop with the stereotypes and superstitions!

This book is a journey into a year and a day exploration into animistic witchcraft, so some part of you the reader is interested in the occult or ways of the witch. By connecting with your primary spirit animal, you are calling upon a familiar to assist you on this journey through a year and a day.

Witches have always been portrayed as having animal companions. Now I am not buying into the witch craze or hysteria that was dominant in the European witch hunts and suggesting that your familiar be given to you by the Devil and that you, in return, will offer it blood from a wart or a mole on your body. No! I am saying that this connection you make with your primary spirit animal will serve as a mirror of who you are and what attributes you are capable of mirroring back to the world around you.

For me personally, I do view wolf as my familiar for the time being. Some days I feel that my connection with wolf is not as dominant and that is when I open myself up for other animals to come through as my teacher, mentor, messenger or guide. But wolf is my PSA (primary spirit animal) and because I am *familiar* with wolf, because of my years of study and devotion, it is easy for me to recognize when I am showing more teeth than the situation may need OR that I am not showing nearly enough.

By taking time to really look into the mirror of one's soul and allow an animalistic side to look back, you create a connection that is not fed by ego or insecurities. That is the power with animism. Please keep in mind that animism is NOT just about seeing the divine in animals, but in ALL things.

Most witches also have a plant familiar and gemstone familiar. Both of these are tangible, physical items that a practicing witch has formulated a strong, working relationship with. These plants, stones and animals become close friends of the witch. These familiars bring about a sense of balance, peace and wholeness. They become a staple in one's day to day practice of the Craft.

What plant do you have a strong relationship with?
What stone do you always go to first?

CHAPTER THREE

Honoring the Animals Reflected in Others

In my first book, *Animals as Gods*, the intention was to really see a connection with the ancient gods/goddesses of old and the animals that were associated with them. Here we have an opportunity to take that practice further and start embracing the animals in each other.

As stated before, my lover is a bear and my familiar is a wolf – two very different animals, with very different needs, communication styles, sleeping patterns, predator and prey aspects. How can two drastically different animals coexist? Well, when we were first married, we had our astrological charts done and they basically told us that we shouldn't even be in the same room together, let alone build a life together.

Our early years were filled with ups and downs like any couple learning to live in the same space and adapt to each other's individual quirks. It was a challenge and at times almost too difficult a challenge to endure. But we are both pretty stubborn and we found a way.

When animism came into to play, it was the bridge that helped us both to overcome our egos and insecurities and see each other in a more loving and accepting way. Instead of automatically reacting to something the other is doing that is very matter of factually NOT how we would do it ourselves, we now flip this switch in our minds that reminds us of each other's individual flare as a totally different species. It works! I know how my inner wolf can be nippy and impatient when his inner bear is a bit stubborn and resistant. But, if we were in the wild, we would never stop each other and demand that wolf become a bear in every aspect, nor can I demand that bear become a wolf. So, we have learned. We have stepped into a space in our relationship that is more accepting and ultimately our relationship has grown stronger because of our PSA's being seen and honored.

How does one accomplish this in the zoo of the world we live in? Well, honestly, if we can all take a step back and remember that we are all individuals coexisting on the same planet and that no two of us are alike, maybe that is a good start.

If you web search 'relationship tips' you will literally come up with hundreds of thousands, if not into the millions, of websites, articles, advice and an onslaught of therapists to assist in how to best enhance your relationships. This can be beyond overwhelming and, let's be honest, by the time you sit down to look into how to best heal your relationship, it is safe to say that your relationship is on the rocks and already struggling.

What's the first step? Communication tips in relationship offers about 221,000,000 results just on Google alone! The way we, as humans, communicate is just not good! We are very rarely taught in our childhood what heartfelt communication is and even more rarely shown was heartfelt listening is. 90% of most conversations is a 'listen to respond' interaction instead of actually listening to what is being said. Then of course we have the defensive listening, avoidance listening and problem solving listening.

As individuals, we all grow up in distinctly different homes, family structures. Then, when we start dating, decide to get married or cohabitate, we take those communication techniques that we were mirrored or taught and implement them into our personal relationships, work relationships and just casual meet and greet on the streets, and it all becomes a cluster fuck! People are offended, shocked, confused and defensive, then emotions take over and any hopes of a decent communication that is actually productive dies right then and there.

So how do we as individuals get past this human attribute of horrible communicating? Well, like I stated, there are millions of steps, tips, websites and such that will offer you tips, but one way to address communication hiccups is to know what animal you are communicating with.

Set a time to offer the PSA meadow of connection meditation to your partner, spouse, work colleague, etc. Then begin the process of getting to know each other as animals. My home is filled with my lover, our two adult children, our teenager and granddaughter – quite literally a zoo!! We have a lion, a bear, a wolf ... a ZOO!!! Each of us communicates differently. Some days we have it down to a science, and others we need to push, pause and really seek clarification.

Now I am not saying that just because your significant other is a large apex predator, that it automatically excuses aggressive communication. No! There is an art to communication, and each animal you live with, have relations with or engage with is 100% accountable for the words spoken, tone of voice and intention behind those words.

Seeing humans as their PSA or animal familiars may just soften the reactionary response and give one time to clarify. For example, if my bear comes across as very boisterous and growling, I can either nip, bark or growl back or I can inquire with a simple, "did you mean to come across as angry and attacking?" Any time we are having a conversation, we are listening to learn, right? When we ask someone "how was your day?" we are wanting to learn how their day was. ... So, we listen.

If you go into the woods to observe animals in their natural habitat, you are making an attempt to learn through observation. You can tell a lot about someone when you observe them. The way someone carries themselves, gestures during a conversation or even when making eye contact. These are the non-verbal ways that the body is conveying what the words are attempting to express.

Animals communicate in four basic ways: visual, auditory, tactile and chemical. When communicating with the zoo in your life, step into a zoosemiotics role (that is a big word that means 'to study animal communication'). By observing how someone is physically moving while communicating, you can tell through their gestures what they are wanting to say without even hearing the verbal message conveyed. An animal will let you know when it is frightened without actually verbally expressing that it is frightened. We do the same thing. But, as humans, we have become so dependent on the verbal skills that we oftentimes miss the other key factors in communicating.

When we apply animal communication to our year and a day, with animals leading the way as teachers, mentors, messengers and guides, we can better understand what lesson we are being taught. For instance, every morning I take my son's dog Gus on a walk. We live in the High Desert and so I keep my eyes peeled open for a chance encounter with an animal guide for my day. When I see a lizard, I take note of its physical communication. Just two mornings ago, we found a horned toad playing dead in the road. This is a defensive mechanism, so I gently picked up the horned toad and moved him into the bushes so he wouldn't get hurt laying in the road. I digested this message from toad to be a reminder that I may have some conflict occur during the day, but it would be best if I did not participate and played dead, so to speak. I also absorbed that I was receiving a message from a reptile with rather thick skin and tough scales, which let me know that I needed to put up an emotional barrier or armor if and when conflict presented itself.

There are numerous ways to interpret animal communication with the humans in your life and the animals that they mirror. What I love about animism in communication is that there is a pause to digest and really seek to learn from what is being communicated, rather than an automatic attack or response.

Another great tip in communication is to not take everything so personally. Not everything is a personal attack. Although, admittedly, poor communication can make it appear that way. As individuals, we have the utmost accountability for how we perceive anything and everything. For some, rattlesnakes are just aggressive no matter what, while, to others, they are magnificently beautiful. They are clear communicators when it comes to their intentions and if you break it down, they rattle to let one know that they are there. A rattlesnake doesn't just strike to strike! In all honesty though, some humans are just aggressive and they do strike to strike with the intent of their words being to hurt. We have the last say though, because we can choose to back away, avoiding the strike and disengage further or we can strike back, letting our emotions take over; which leads to us both being energetically and emotionally punctured.

HONORING THE ANIMALS REFLECTED IN OTHERS

Accountability is huge in everything we choose to engage in when it comes to all types of conversing. Be ever mindful of your inner predator and inner prey when it comes to uncomfortable communications. ... Ask yourself, "what am I really wanting to express?"

When we honor the animals reflected back in others, we create a space for others to be their full selves, free from judgment and expectations. By knowing what animal vibrates with those you come into contact with, it opens more than just the doors to communication; it helps to uncover needs that the individual may not feel comfortable with or even aware of enough to openly share.

Sleep patterns and the need for sleep are different for everyone. Some people with certain PSA's require more sleep and often tend to nap more. For example, people who have a cat (domestic or exotic) for their primary spirit animal, seem to require more sleep. As wolf, I require very little sleep. Don't get me wrong, I enjoy sleep but I am always on alert; my ears pricked listening for sounds in the night. My sleep is very rarely deep and peaceful. I have an insane amount of energy and when I am up, I am up and ready to go. My bear, on the other hand, sleeps very deeply and it's often difficult to wake him. If he does get woken up, he is slow to get going or rather growly.

Physical affection is another thing that, in the past decade of doing animism with the focus on connecting people to their PSA, I have noticed is very similar to the needs of the actual animal a person is reflecting back. Big cats and little cats (exotic or domestic) love affection and will demand it when they want it and make known when they don't. It is a common joke that ALL cats still remember that they were once worshipped as gods and still, in this modern world, they expect their human caregivers to bow down to their needs.

People with cats as their PSA like to cuddle, lounge about and play with their hair. I know it sounds silly, but I have seen it so many times. When I had an active coven, one of the requirements when someone joined it was to have their animal connection meditation done so that I knew what animal I was working with. At one point in my coven, we had seven big cats!!! Coven meetings became cuddle parties, playing with each other's hair and, if they were interrupted, then a hiss of protest would occur.

Like it or not we are mammals, we are instinctual. As humans, we have the ability to speak and formulate sentences; I'm not entirely sure if this is a positive trait in today's world. But we do have some advantages over our animal kingdom comrades. Or are these disadvantages? How we relate to each other can become a very empowering exchange when we drop the ego, expectations and obligations we enforce upon each other. If we start seeing each other as animals, would that change how we interact with each other? I think it would! I have seen it! Even if we take away the animal connection, if we started allowing people their own authentic quirks and stopped expecting them to fit our acceptance molds, things would shift dramatically. Can we do that? Getting along in today's world seems a very unlikely possibility but, as an optimist, I believe it can happen. Animals just may be the link.

Some questions often asked when I do couples' animal connecting are: "What happens if we are totally different species? What if one of us is an insect and the other one a bird that is known to eat that insect?" With the different species question, I simply remind the couple that they already are different species. Remember the book that came out in the early 90's, *Men are from Mars, Women are from Venus*? Well, that book basically said the same thing; that men and women are totally different species from the beginning. We are raised differently and have a different chemical makeup. So yes, we are different species.

Now things have progressed since the 90's and gender has become more fluid and open. We can no longer use excuses like, "Well you're just saying that because you are a man and you are from Mars." Or, "That's just what Venetian women do." NO! We have adapted and grown. While the book is good and served a purpose for the time that it was released, we as humans are adapting to the world around us at a rapid rate and it's time to break free from those gender confines and stigmas and be more fluid. We are all different species! So yes, we are all going to have totally different and unique PSA's come through when we make the connection in the meadow.

Now, as to the second question about an insect and a bird eating that insect as dinner, my response is often, "In which ways do you feel like you are the prey and being attacked?" This opens the door up for communication and allows some real honest feelings to be expressed.

I will never forget the time I did a group animal connection meditation at a three-day women's weekend retreat. My niece, who was very much exploring her sexuality and contemplating lesbianism, had embraced a matriarchal, 'damn the man' attitude and her PSA that came through in meditation was a praying mantis. She was irate! She stormed out of the goddess temple and threw a literal fit. Now I should say that my niece is very tall and lanky and when she told the group about the connection, she made me laugh, out loud! She looked like a praying mantis and she was very much in the mood to bite off the head of the next male that spoke to her.

My favorite thing about offering animal connection to large groups is seeing everyone's reaction to each other. Especially when they observe that there are physical similarities with the person and the animal that comes through as their PSA. I wouldn't say I look like a wolf, but I have come to realize that I do have some pronounced canine teeth (well actually it was pointed out to me that when I am contemplating something or about to pounce in attack mode, I quite literally lick my chops). I had a dear friend whose PSA was a raven and she would sit perched on the edge of any chair she sat on with her feet on the edge and her knees up under her chin. When she was excitedly telling a story, she would talk in a chirping sing-song manner with her head cocking from one angle to the next. It was always fascinating to watch and it let me know what kind of mood she was in.

If we think of dogs and their ability to just know if someone is a good person or not simply by the way they approach, why can't we do the same? We are capable of observing the body language and gestures of others, but do we put the two together as behavioral clues as to what kind of mood the person is in or whether or not they have good intentions.

As humans who have darted down the rabbit hole of narcissism and social media, we have lost the ability to activate our guttural response, because we don't have to. Communication and engagement with others is primarily happening with a screen separating us. We are able in the social media world to literally recreate a completely new persona and present only what we want others to see and share only what we can control. We have embraced a new way to have community but there is harm in this world of screens and technology. While we feel safer, this mentality of avoidance and separation is damaging our instincts. While the world repairs, we have to learn to step out of our comfort zones, our Zoom circles and classes, and we have to interact with each other.

Remember that scene in the movie, *Mean Girls*, where Cady goes primal in the cafeteria which then causes everyone else to go primal as if they are in a jungle attack scene? Well life is like that, more often than not. We are literally attacking each other all the time! Why? Did we forget that we were all taught to be unique and strive to be ourselves? When we compare ourselves to others, we enter a state of competing. When we compete, we defeat. Animal work is so powerful because how can we compare ourselves when our PSA's are so drastically different? As a wolf, I honor that and my lover is a bear, which I honor. I don't look at him and wish he was a wolf or that I was a bear. By seeing the connection we have when we mirror our PSA's, we are not only welcoming the authenticity in each other, but we are celebrating it through love and allowance.

Knowing the PSA of those around us helps tremendously in moving forward in relationships because we can understand better the individual's behavior, character, diet and social status. For example, if you are a pack animal, like me, and you are establishing a connection with someone whose PSA is a spider, you may have some learning curves when it comes to going out and mingling, as those who connect with spider tend to be very solitary, creative and focused people.

Can we learn to adapt and be fluid with each other, even though we have totally different species for our PSA's? Yes! We can and it should be easier because we are not imposing the human ego of expectations. Rather, we are enacting the human desire to love, honor and respect animals. ... Even spirit animals.

There is an article on the *whatismyspiritanimal.com* website titled, "How to Find your Soulmate by Using Spirit Animal Alchemy." I love the word 'alchemy'! The dictionary offers this definition of alchemy: "A seemingly magical process of transformation, creation, or combination." Combining this word with spirit animal is just tantalizing!

In the article, the author, Bernadette King, takes you through a meditation to meet your spirit animal soulmate. My favorite line of the article is, "As soulmates, we agree to come in and out of each other's lifetimes so we can each learn and grow as divine beings." Love is a beautiful thing. When you take totally unique individuals that seem to have nothing in common, and eliminate the prejudices of expectations and stipulations, you can experience a real love that knows no limits.

https://whatismyspiritanimal.com/spirit-animal-quiz/

How can knowing one's PSA assist in a year and a day journey? While you may not have physical access to animals in the wild, you do have people around you all of the time that can offer you their animal mirror. The only limits we have in life are those that we choose to place on ourselves. When it comes to making animism the core of one's year and a day journey, one has to be open to the guidance in the liminal spaces, the in-between and the unpredictable.

Often in the morning when I am out walking, I am keeping my eyes open for animal messengers and guides. This morning, a herd of antelope crossed my walking path and the elder of the herd and I exchanged a real heart-to-heart moment where he stood and stared me down, letting me know this was his family and I was not to come any closer. This boundary that he set was to be respected.

EXERCISE OF AWARENESS

For just a moment, gift yourself with some breathwork. Close your eyes and inhale to the count of four and exhale to the count of four. Allow your physical body to release any tension or stresses within as you exhale them out and away. Feel how your body becomes heavy, soft and ultimately relaxed.

Now move into your mind, tap into that imagination and see yourself in a room filled with people. This can be your workplace, your home, church, a bar, the grocery store, etc. See the people all around you going about their business. Now see them as animals.

JOURNAL PROMPT

What did it feel like seeing the humans shift into animals in a normal day to day setting?

This exercise is simple and it gives you permission to leave ego mind and step into the realm of *all things are possible if you only believe.* We can shift our interactions with the people around us if we rise above ego and see things with a new perspective, see others through new lenses.

We can step into a more open minded way of living in our communities by being consciously aware of how we view each other and interact with each other. We all know puppy people. Those people who go insane when they see a puppy! The excitement, the childlike adoration and the need to want to pet the puppy. We all know people like that. Well, what if we allowed others to see us as through the animal mirror we reflect and honor the animal reflected back? Not everyone likes wolves, I know I didn't when wolf first came through. I know that, for those who sense my wolf energy, they are usually going to react with hesitation to approach me, which is preferred; I like to have boundaries. Through time though, they know that if they allow an interaction with me, I really am just a big puppy that wants my butt scratched so to speak. So, my challenge for you is to step outside of your norm and, for just a moment, when you are engaged in conversation with someone, close your eyes and when you open them, see if you can see their animal looking back at you.

CHAPTER FOUR

The Wheel of the Year

The Wiccan Wheel of the Year has its origins in the work of Margaret Murray, Gerald Gardner and Aidan Kelly. During the 1920's, Murray developed a calendar based on ancient Pagan festival rites. This calendar was further refined by Gerald Gardner during the 1950's. Gardner added solstices, equinoxes and incorporated elements of Celtic fire festivals into the calendar. It is Aidan Kelly who is credited with giving the calendar its name: 'Wheel of the Year,' during the 1970's.

As the wheel turns, the seasons change. The Wheel of the Year is by definition "an annual cycle of seasonal festivals observed by many modern Pagans." These festivals consist of solstices and equinoxes and the midpoints between. Some refer to the Wheel of the Year as a Celtic calendar. This reference is pretty broad! With the goal and objective of embracing Wicca, witchcraft and a more Pagan-centered way of life being to realign once more with Nature, what better way than to celebrate the turning of the great wheel that we live on?

The Wheel of the Year consists of four Gaelic fire festivals, known as Samhain (sow-en), Imbolc (silent b), Beltane and Lughnasadh (loo-nas-ah). When these fire festivals are combined with the winter solstice (Yule), spring equinox (Ostara), summer solstice (Litha), autumn equinox (Mabon); you get the Wheel of the Year.

These eight Pagan holidays, or seasonal sabbats, celebrate a change in season or a mid-point, with each being evenly split throughout the year. It should be noted that the Southern Hemisphere has all the seasonal sabbats and solstices inverted. For example, when the Northern Hemisphere is celebrating Yule, the Southern Hemisphere is celebrating Litha. If you choose to honor the Wheel of the Year in your home and your Solitary practice, honor where you live.

In our home, we honor the Wheel of the Year as our calendar of holidays and festivities that mark changes, not only in the agricultural aspect, but also the seasons within ourselves. For many Pagans, the Wheel of the Year is a mirror and reminder that we, as humans, cycle and go through changes seasonally.

The foundation of a Pagan practice begins with the understanding and willingness to embrace that we are not separate from Nature; we are a part of Nature. When we walk, talk, eat and live seasonally, as a mirror of what Nature is doing, then we can begin to shift our consciousness to a more Nature-conscious existence where we physically, emotionally and spiritually feel the seasons, Wheel of the Year and the sabbats move through us.

My calendar of the year begins on the first day of November, making Samhain our New Year's Eve. Samhain (pronounced 'sow-en' although, if you do say Samhain, no worries – most kind hearted Pagans will know what you are talking about and won't feel the need to correct you) is the largest celebration of the year in our home. Some refer to Samhain as All Hallows' Eve, Halloween and/or the Witches' New Year. However you choose to celebrate and honor the seasons really is up to you.

Pagans are NOT members of any Abrahamic religion and thereby do not have access to a "how to practice, live, eat or celebrate manual." No offence if you are Christian; I am merely pointing out that, for Pagans, there is no book or set scriptures that dictate how we are to live our practice. We follow instead, depending on which tradition we honor, our instinctual and intuitive connection with the elements, seasons and Nature in a very individual way and manner. For some that are welcomed into, initiated by or facilitating a coven or grove, there may be a more defined and organized, structured way of honoring one's path and the celebrating the Wheel of the Year.

Each seasonal sabbat on the Wheel of the Year contains certain elemental characteristics, deities, foods, celebrations, rituals and animals that correspond, compliment and create the uniqueness of each holiday.

For example, Samhain is a time when the veil that separates the living from the dead drops and the dead walk amongst us. It is a time of great mystery and occult magic. We are all too familiar with the symbols, décor and ambiance of All Hallows' from pumpkins, ghosts, witches, zombies, vampires and an incredible list that can go on and on.

In our home, we celebrate Samhain by having an ancestral feast and séance. The dinner is set and all the candles in the home are lit. We eat the most amazing decadent dinner of the entire year and we call upon the recently deceased ancestors, then we call to the ancestors that we wish to connect with and invite them into our home. This is the night that we set our intentions for the New Year ahead, asking the ancestors to guide us and to walk with us into the New Year.

By living a more seasonally conscious life, one's solitary journey and activation into witchcraft becomes a sustainable, activation of connection with Nature. When we can sense the change of season blowing in the breeze or smell the leaves as they begin to dry out in preparation for their *fall*, we too can sense within how we are changing. The Wheel of the Year is a guide, a blueprint a calendar of what's next.

JOURNAL PROMPT

What's your favorite time of year? Why? Do you have a favorite seasonal celebration? Why? Make a list of everything you do and love about that particular Season and Event. Be detailed. What is happening outside, which foods are in Season, what meals do you love to prepare and consume, which traditions do you have, or would like to create, what are the animals doing this time of year?

Step into a more observation-based role and then add a bit of your own magick. How can you create a ritual that honors this season or how can you amplify an already existing ritual or celebration?

A GLANCE AT THE SEASONAL SABBATS' UNIQUE ATTRIBUTES

Samhain
Colors – orange, yellow, red, black.
Animals – bats, spiders, werewolves, black cats.

Festivities – trick-or-treating, feasting, costume parties.
Plants – pumpkins, squash.

Yule
Colors – red, green, gold, silver, white.
Animals – reindeer.
Festivities – gift giving, caroling, Yule feasting, dinner parties.
Plants – mistletoe, pine, evergreen, holly.

Imbolc
Colors – green, white, pale yellow.
Animals – lamb, swan.
Festivities – making candles, feasting, bread baking.
Plants – pussy willow, daffodil, crocus.

Ostara
Colors – pastel pink, blue, green, yellow.
Animals – bunnies, chicks, baby animals of all kinds.
Festivities – egg dying, egg hunting, feasting.
Plants – crocus, daffodil, lilies, dandelions.

Beltane
Colors – red, green, white, orange, yellow.
Animals – goats, deer, butterflies, rabbits, bees.
Festivities – dancing of the maypole, bonfires, making flower crowns, feasting.
Plants – rosemary, mint, tulips, all flowers.

Litha
Colors – yellow, orange, gold, red, bronze, green.
Animals – bees, cow, butterflies, dragonflies, horse, deer, songbirds.
Festivities – sunbathing, bonfires, feasting, picnics.
Plants – daisy, marigold, basil, rosemary, sage.

Lughnasadh
Colors – yellow, orange, blue, gold, red.
Animals – dragonflies, lizards, stag, eagle, crow, salmon.
Festivities – bread baking, feasting, making corn dollies.
Plants – all summer flowers, wheat, sunflowers, mugwort.

Mabon
Colors – red, yellow, orange, brown, gold, bronze.
Animals – owl, raven, wolf.
Festivities – harvest feast, harvesting the garden, bonfires.
Plants – squashes, sunflowers, acorns, pumpkins.

This is just a sampling of the things that correspond with each seasonal sabbat. If you want to journey down the rabbit hole of Pinterest, you will find an onslaught of already crafted correspondence sheets for each sabbat.

Notice that in my brief samplings, I did not include deities, stone people (crystals) or magical properties for each sabbat. The focus of this book is really how to utilize animals as the focal point rather than the gods. For, though I have said it before, it's worth repeating; most new-to-the-Craft witches are healing from patriarchy, and oftentimes working with a god or goddess can be a struggle, but almost everyone can appreciate animals. If you are wanting to make a strong connection between animals and the god or goddess they correspond with, you can reference my first book, *Animals as Gods*, for a glimpse.

Knowing the basics of what attributes are associated with each sabbat is a good jumping-off point. I found it especially helpful when setting altars or planning large community gatherings. The key really is one's own unique connection and experience with the seasons. Let's dive into that for a bit.

Spring, summer, fall and winter. We are all familiar with the seasons whether we experience all of them in full swing or not. Where I live, it is not uncommon to experience all four in an afternoon. Sometimes I wonder if this High Desert in Southern Utah is a bit confused. When it comes to the seasons, we all have our favorites and we all have reasons why they are our favorite.

For me I love fall (autumn). When I wake up and there is a crisp in the morning breeze and the smell of leaves fills the air, it automatically makes me want to grab a blanket, some warm coffee and read a good book on the patio. Fall for me means celebration. The year is winding down, the garden is at its peak with harvest and food preparation following. Then of course there are all the delicious foods, from pies and ciders, to freshly baked breads and plenty of squash!!

Through the years, as I have grown into a more seasoned witch and embraced animism as my foundation, I have found that there are things I absolutely love and look forward to in all of the seasons and there are things that I do not enjoy but know they will pass and, soon enough, a new season will arrive. Being consciously aware and knowing that I am one with Nature allows me a space for the seasons to move through me as me. So while we touched on the correspondences that are common with each sabbat and season, there are still quite a lot of emotional correspondences that surface as well.

Just like in the fall, I know that I can reflect on what I have gained; the energetic seeds that were planted in the spring and tended to in the summer. Fall gives me time to reap the rewards of hard work. It also gives me time to prepare and focus on the dark of the year which is winter. Internally, we vibrate and move with the seasons, just like the animals do. Let's take a look at how the animals move through the Wheel of the Year based upon the four seasons. After all, the Wheel of the Year and its seasonal sabbats is based on the four seasons.

CORRESPONDING ANIMALS FOR THE SEASONS

Spring – robins, bees, butterflies, songbirds, frogs, bears, lambs, sheep, ladybugs, geese, rabbits, hares, chicks, earthworms, gophers, groundhogs, prairie dogs, hummingbirds, fawns, baby birds of all kinds.

For me, I know spring has officially arrived when I see robins in the yard. They are the ones that herald in the new life and energy of the season. Spring is all about new beginnings. Baby animals are born in the spring, birds are hatching and the mornings are alive with the chatter of songbirds. It's no wonder that springtime is filled with joy as thoughts of hope, love and playfulness fill the air.

Spring is also associated with the archetype of the maiden and the page. Both young aspects of the Divine Feminine and the Divine Masculine coming out of their winter slumber to explore and play.

What energetic seeds and physical seeds do you plant in the spring?

Summer – lizards, flies, butterflies, bees, wasps, mosquitoes, horses, deer, ravens, eagles, lions, dragons, cows, snakes, songbirds, foxes, coyotes, wolves, bears, antelope. ...

Think of animals that need the heat of the Sun to survive and you will surely see them out sunbathing in the warmth of the summer sun. When the herd of antelope appears in my desert landscape, I know summer has finally arrived. What a treat to see how many new ones were born in the spring. Summer is when the garden is buzzing, literally with all things that buzz!

Summer is all about thriving! Playing! Getting outside and enjoying Nature. Going on hikes, boating on the lake and pretty much anything that takes you out of the office and into the great outdoors. Summer is all about heat and passion for life. The baby animals from spring have grown and they are becoming daring young teenagers who want to explore, play and experience life and their surroundings. Summer is a time for travels and breaking free.

Summer is also associated with the archetype of the mother and the knight. With the focus being passion, it's no wonder that there is a frisky sense of sexuality in the air. Knight energy is all about taking risks and running towards things that are exciting. While the mother aspect combines that passion and propels the need to create joy in the moment and to give birth to the sparks that are inside of us that will turn into a bonfire of self expression and authenticity. How do you embrace the heat of summer?

Fall – dragonflies, ants, owls, foxes, squirrels, chipmunks, skunks, wolves, groundhogs, bears, deer, goats, sheep, cows, horses. …

Fall is the time when animals and people who live hand in hand with the land begin to reap the rewards of the harvest. Crops are gathered, stored and preserved. Animals are taking advantage of the summer abundance and, come the fall, they have begun to gather nuts, berries, seeds, etc to build stock that will make sure they survive the winter.

They also consume ample amounts of the harvest to ensure they have enough fat reserves to keep them warm and thriving in the approaching months of winter.

Fall is associated with the archetypes of the queen and kings; they who rule over their kingdoms and provide not just for themselves but for their kingdoms. As an avid gardener, fall is a busy time and consists of quite a bit of work outdoors in order to properly make use of the plants grown and to prepare for the winter.

As an herbalist and green witch, I spend about three days every other week harvesting, drying, making salves, bundles and teas from the herbs in my herb garden. From the vegetable garden, I spend time drying, bottling, canning and baking. How do you prepare for winter in the fall?

Winter – caribou, reindeer, wolves, snow owls, polar bears, musk oxen, snow leopards, arctic hares, arctic foxes, penguins, rams, Yule goat. …

Winter where I live is cold! We get below freezing quite often and it's not unusual to have a high of five degrees. We rely upon the heat from a wood burning stove and since I am not a 'snow bunny' (animal pun intended), most of the winter months I am indoors. With the hustle and bustle of the garden at rest for the season, winter is a time for inward focus. Soaking up the last bits of energetic seeds and intentions that were set at the beginning of the spring, reading lots of books, creating artwork and doing things that create a calm sense of wonder.

Winter is not my favorite season but there is a pure kind of magick that comes with the first snow fall that is undeniable. It's as if Mother Nature has tucked us all in under her majestic blanket of white and she says: "rest now." The quiet calm of winter has become something that I look forward to.

Winter is associated with the crone and sage; the elders in the archetype. The ones who have learned to slow down and take inventory of their life, share their stories with the youth in the hopes that they will learn and not repeat past mishaps.

I often connect winter with the Hermit card from the Tarot; that old wise seeker who withdraws from the chaos and sends focus inwards in deep soul searching. The Hermit card is linked to the Old Norse All-Father, Odin; "He who wanders in search of great knowledge." I adore Odin energy and winter is all about Odin, but that is a story for another book. Winter is a great time to retreat and look within.

We all live through the seasons and experience them in similar circumstances, despite living in different climates. We can all relate to the energetic shift of the planet because we all live on the same planet.

When we begin to slow down and look around us, the animals have been teaching us and walking as our guides since the beginning. Remember that the first humans had animals to look to as teachers of where to find food, water, what to eat and what not to eat. Animals were the ones that provided them with food, fur for warmth and showed them where to hunt and how to hunt.

The early hunters and gatherers were foragers whose sole survival relied upon animals as guides and sources of food. One's personal and collective relationship with the local environment meant literal survival for the individual and the tribe. Animals were both the guides and the means for that survival. While in today's world, we do not need to rely on consuming meat like our ancestors, as we have learned to adapt and with medical advances, we now can basically itemize our pantries based off a variety of personal health needs. Our ancestors have taught us that animals and their instinctual survival skills are vital for our survival as humans.

THE ANIMALS THAT TURN THE SEASONS WITH THEIR ACTIONS

Spring – birds (song of welcome to longer days).
Summer – lizards (rely upon the power of the Sun to live).
Fall – squirrels (gather, store and be prepared).
Winter – bears (slow down, retreat, hibernate).

CHAPTER FIVE

Signs and Symbols throughout the Year

Plants, animals and humans all shift and change along with the seasons. We are masters of adapting. When the snow begins to melt, the days begin to grow longer and the plants begin to push through their once frozen blanket to find the warmth of the Sun. The insects awaken and the animals that rely upon these newly awakened plants and insects begin to wake up from their winter sleep as well. When all members of the food chain have plenty of food, they thrive!

Animals have learned that in the springtime and summer there is plenty of food for themselves and their young. They can survive. However, if they were to wait until the winter to reproduce, their chance of survival for their species would be risky if not detrimental. Animals hone into their instinctual environmental cues which are circumstances that inform the animal of what is occurring in their local landscape and how to react to that. For example, if an animal's food source is thriving, they too will thrive. If it is diminishing, then they know to stock up on reserves in order to survive.

One major environmental cue is sunlight which determines the length of each day. Chickens, for example, need at least six hours of sunlight in order to lay eggs. Songbirds are very sensitive and knowledgeable on the amount of sunlight in each season, which is why they lay their eggs in the spring, which ensures that their young will survive due to the increase of sunlight in the summer months providing ample amount of food for their fledglings. If they were to hatch eggs in the fall, their young would not have enough food sources to survive.

Our ancestors lived off the land – they were actively engaged in creating their own survival. So when a herd of animals that they relied upon for food began to migrate, they too would migrate, following the animals. "Our artificial environment protects us from most cues to seasonal changes in the natural environment, such as changes in light and temperature. This may mean that we miss the environmental triggers that would regulate any biological seasonal cycles that do exist." While this quote is spot on, I would argue with the word *'protects'* as I personally feel our society and humankind in general would benefit from stepping outside more and not relying so much on this 'artificial environment' that we have become spoiled by and, in essence, separated from Nature.

While the signs and symbols are literally everywhere pointing to animals as ever present and diligent teachers, masters and guides; from each yoga asana being named after an animal, to the Tarot being filled with animals, to our astrological signs of the zodiac – animals have been walking beside us faithfully since our first breaths.

To actively live the Wheel of the Year, we need to begin by honoring that each year is a day by day journey through not just the physical seasons, but the seasons within us as individuals. This will create an energetic, spiritual and physical shift that will allow our lives to become more harmonious, conscious and empowered.

Take a brief inventory of your day. How do you begin? Are you irritated? Tired? In a rush? Now look at birds – how do they begin their day? Not everyone is a morning person, but birds have much to teach us if we will just stop and observe. Everyone is familiar with the phrase "the early bird gets the worm." Well there is truth to that! Creating a daily devotion and starting your day as an intentional creator of your existence is one way to shift consciousness.

How about your afternoons? Your evenings? How are you actively engaged in your life? How are you actively present? Or are you just going through the motions? With witchcraft, Paganism and Wicca being the fastest growing practices on the planet, it's safe to say that, collectively, we as humans are longing for more and realizing that our technological advances have not given us the peace of mind that our ancestors had. The Earth is a wheel that turns and we are turning with it; but are we actively engaged in that turning?

There are so many tools within our grasp, signs and symbols everywhere. We just need to open our eyes and see that the teachers have been with us all along. For example, the Tarot is a tool that has become increasingly popular within the past decade and it is full of animal messengers and insight to create a more intuitively present life.

THE ANIMALS THAT TURN THE WHEEL OF FORTUNE

The Tarot is the most commonly used divination tool by witches, Pagans and Wiccans. While there are still very intense misconceptions surrounding the Tarot and in some parts of the world and the United States it is illegal to use Tarot as a means of fortune-telling, it is an effective tool and the symbolism found within can be life-changing as well as inspiring.

When it comes to animals as guides who walk us through the Wheel of the Year, we can't ignore the presence of their messages found within the Tarot. The Wheel of Fortune card, much like the popular game show that shares its name, is an example of how the animals really do turn the wheel of not just the calendar year, but of life itself.

Let's look at the symbols shall we? We see an angel, eagle, bull, lion, snake, sphinx and a red fox-like devil character who is a representative of Anubis himself (the Great Jackal God). Within the center of the image, you see a wheel that looks incredibly similar to the Celtic Wheel of the Year, with letters and symbols. The letters themselves spell out 'Tarot'. So what do these all mean?

On this card, we see the four fixed astrological signs in the corners of the card. In the north is the bull of Taurus, in the south we see the lion of Leo, the angel of Aquarius in the east and the eagle (phoenix) in the west. These four quarter guardians have also been adopted by Christianity as the four Evangelists with Luke the Taurean bull of Earth, Scorpio/eagle as John of the water, Matthew as Aquarian man of air and the lion of fire being Mark.

There is so much symbolism in this single image that you can be richly fed off just this one card alone. The most important essence is the wheel in the center, which depicts and showcases the cyclic nature of life that we all live, determined by the seasons and turning of the great wheel.

With the sphinx on the top showing us stability in chaos as the wheel turns, we are offered the power of self-accountability when it comes to raising the sword of thought and cutting through all the fog to bring about clarity. The snake, which some may see as having similarities with the serpent from the Garden of Eden who tempts Eve with the forbidden fruit of the tree of knowledge of good and evil, represents choices. Anubis or the devil-like character shows us good fortune and success.

Each of the four characters/animals on the corners shows us the elemental connections as well as emotional attributes. Such as, east being intellect, west emotions, south passion and north possessions. They are also each holding a book that really shows wisdom.

Animal messages and symbolism is everywhere within the Tarot from the bull, horse, cat, dog, ram, birds, lobster, lion, lizard, rabbit, snake and turtle to the wolf. But it's not just the Tarot! In many methods of divination, we are guided by animals, for they are the most common subjects that show up! It is very common in tea leaves, oracular and dreamwork for animals to come through as guides.

Animals literally come to us in one way or another every day! The key is seeing them as masters, teachers and guides. Then we need to honor the fact that we are mammals as well and thereby we are animals, so it makes sense that our kin are showing us how to survive!

THE WHEEL OF THE YEAR

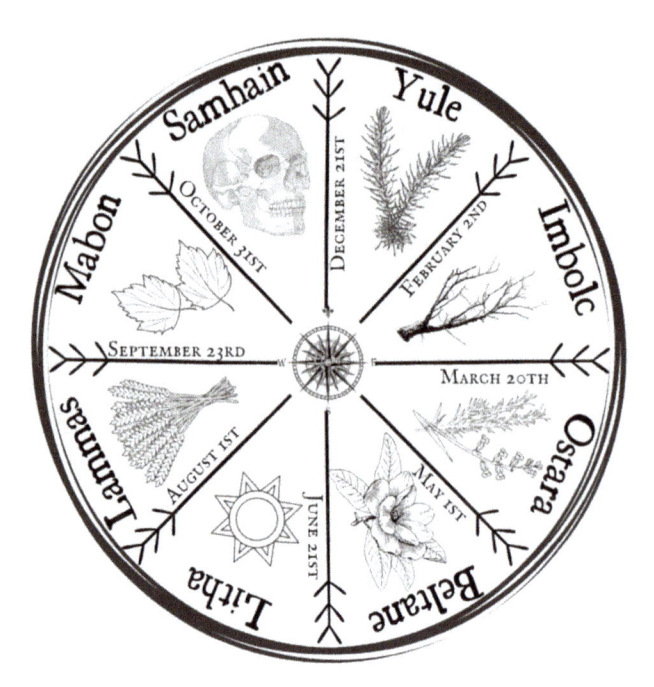

https://divinationandfortunetelling.com/articles/2018/7/2/ meanings-of-animal-symbols-on-tarot-cards

ANIMALS WITHIN THE ZODIAC SIGNS

Between 500 BCE to around 1300 BCE, the zodiac signs slowly became ever present in the world. They originate from the Akkadians and Sumerians of Mesopotamia who created the Bull of Taurus, Crab of Cancer, Moon Goddess Virgo, Scorpion of Scorpio, Goat of Capricorn and the Fisherman of Pisces. Later to add the Ram of Aries, the Twins of Gemini, Lion of Leo, Scales of Libra, Archer of Sagittarius, and even later would add the Water Bearer of Aquarius.

The zodiac signs were originally used to mark the seasons. Later they were connected to the position of planets and the Moon, when the Greeks used the Babylonian's system for astronomical and astrological reasons. In ancient Greek, the words *zodiakos kyklos* mean 'cycle' or 'circle of animals'.

The Chinese zodiac is different because, while there are twelve signs, they are all represented by animals unlike the Greeks, who utilize part animal and part human. The Chinese zodiac animal is based on the year one was born rather than the date and month. This year is defined by the Chinese lunar calendar, not the Gregorian one that most people are familiar with.

If you think of this planet like a great wheel or sphere, always turning, then you can see why the zodiac comes into play in our lives. "The signs are derived from the constellations that mark out the path on which the Sun appears to travel over the course of a year. Over the course of a year, the Sun appears to be in front of or 'in' different constellations." For example, one month the Sun may be in Cancer, and then the next month in Leo.

It should be noted that the zodiacs we know of today are based on of the Sun's rotation about 2000 years ago and, with time, things have shifted and that includes the wheel we live upon.

When we work with and become acquainted with the animals that correspond with the twelve signs of the zodiac, we can better understand the motions of the Sun, Earth and even our ancestors. The zodiac is a great tool for seeing the mirror of certain attributes corresponding with certain individuals and their PSA (primary spirit animal) and the seasons, both within and around.

My son was born when the Sun was in Cancer and believe me, there are numerous occasions where he is a bit 'crabby'. I personally am a Scorpio and trust me, when my stinger comes out, you know it! Probably should have seen it coming sooner but regardless, you will feel the sting. Our personalities really do reflect our zodiac signs, just like our personalities reflect our PSA's; the similarities can be quite eye-opening but typically always spot on!

Astrologically speaking, one's sun sign highlights the individual's personality, while one's moon sign shows emotions and inner mood. To determine what your sun and moon signs are, you will need the date of your birth, time and location. One's rising sign or 'ascending time' (which reflects your outward personality) is determined by what time of day you were born; before or after the dawn. To break it all down; the sun sign is the center of oneself, the moon sign is one's inner most self and the rising sign is what others see.

The internet has made finding one's zodiac simple! You can literally print off an entire chart in less than five minutes. Just make sure you have your time of birth. My favorite websites are:

www.astrologycafe.com
www.cafeastrology.com
www.astrosofa.com

If the zodiac is based upon the rotation of the Sun through the constellations and planets, then spending time connecting with them will only amplify one's personal journey through the year and the seasons. To assist you in your quest of learning from the animals that represent you based upon your birth month or year, I have included a few lists below:

Sun Sign

Scorpion: Scorpio (October 24th–November 21st)
Archer: Sagittarius (November 22nd–December 21st)
Goat: Capricorn (December 22nd–January 19th)
Water Bearer: Aquarius (January 20th–February 19th)
Fish: Pisces (February 20th–March 20th)
Ram: Aries (March 21st–April 19th)
Bull: Taurus (April 20th–May 20th)
Twins: Gemini (May 21st–June 21st)
Crab: Cancer (June 22nd–July 22nd)
Lion: Leo (July 23rd–Aug 22nd)
Virgin: Virgo (Aug 23rd–September 22nd)
Scales: Libra (September 23rd–October 23rd)

Chinese Zodiac Animals

As stated earlier, the Chinese zodiac consists of twelve animals determined by the lunar calendar. The animals are assigned based on their attributes and repeat every twelve years. These can also be assigned to one month of the year.

Rat (December 5th–January 5th)
Ox (January 6th–February 3rd)
Tiger (February 4th–March 5th)
Rabbit (March 6th–April 5th)
Dragon (April 6th–May 5th)

Snake (May 6th–June 5th)
Horse (June 6th–July 5th)
Sheep (July 6th–August 5th)
Monkey (August 6th–September 5th)
Rooster (September 6th–October 5th)
Dog (October 6th–November 5th)
Pig (November 6th–December 5th)

https://www.travelchinaguide.com/intro/social_customs/zodiac/

JUST FOR FUN – STAR SIGNS AND THEIR ANIMALS

This list was found on the *www.animalwised.com* website and was actually quite fascinating. When you read through their descriptions you can really see "how the animal kingdom represents many human personalities and characters." While I would never have thought of linking penguin to Scorpion after digesting the article I could not deny the similarities.

Aquarius - Owl	**Leo** - Lion
Pisces - Dolphin	**Virgo** - Elephant
Aries - Lynx	**Libra** - Fox
Taurus - Horse	**Scorpio** - Penguin
Gemini - Chameleon	**Sagittarius** - Hummingbird
Cancer - Otter	**Capricorn** - Crow

JUST FOR FUN – MY OWN COMPILATION BASED UPON MY EXPERIENCE WITH INDIVIDUALS AND KNOWLEDGE OF ANIMALS AS MIRRORS

Aquarius - Raven	**Leo** - Lion
Pisces - Cat	**Virgo** - Cow
Aries - Eagle	**Libra** - Horse
Taurus - Bear	**Scorpio** - Wolf
Gemini - Chimpanzee	**Sagittarius** - Stag
Cancer - Sloth	**Capricorn** - Coyote

SUPER FUN JOURNAL PROMPT

Spending time collecting the zodiac signs of each member of your extended family makes for more excitement. Then, based on your knowledge of each individual's characteristics and attributes, link them with an animal that would mirror those same attributes. The last step is to combine the two and see if the animal you selected reflects the zodiac.

This is a fun game to play at a large family reunion. This exercise also disconnects you from focusing on the human traits and allows you step into the world of shapeshifting. By seeing others as having similarities with animals, you can drop the guard of ego and begin to relate to each other in a state of love and acceptance. When we can see the animals within, we move away from judgment and comparisons which only feed competition, and we become animists.

CHAPTER SIX

Seasonal Sabbat Animal Guides

Most sabbats include a feast and ceremony or ritual dedicated to a god and goddess (masculine and feminine). The intent with this chapter is to highlight animals that are not commonly known to be associated with the eight seasonal sabbats and spotlight them instead.

Once again, I will express that, for some individuals, making intention to connect energetically and spiritually with a deity can be difficult. Those who are healing from a heavy patriarchal religious background seem to have the most difficulty in doing any kind of devotion that includes a masculine god. I know I did! I steered clear from any masculine deity for the first fifteen years of my practice. By taking time to intentionally focus on an animal in place of a deity, one can step into intense healing.

Those who are non-binary or transitioning find it oftentimes painful to have the main focus of such a beautiful turning of the wheel celebration turn its focus on what at first glance appears to be physical gender. To create a more fluid and open friendly ritual space, the focus of these seasonal sabbats has been shifted to a particular animal being called upon for each sabbat in place of a god or goddess. For each sabbat, you will find obscure animals that are actually connected with the deities commonly associated with the eight seasonal sabbats.

Let's take some time and get to know our eight seasonal animals that will assist us in our Wheel of the Year journey. In the next chapter, you will combine the animal with ceremony.

Samhain - Owl	**Beltane** - Butterflies
Yule - Reindeer	**Summer Solstice** - Hummingbird
Imbolc - Bear	**Lughnasadh** - Eagle
Ostara - Hare	**Mabon** - Salmon

OWL OF SAMHAIN

Samhain/All Hallows'/Halloween is my most favorite sabbat and highest of most high holy days.

Literally months are spent planning for this turn of the wheel, for it is the end of my calendar year and I want to make sure I end each year with intention and merriment.

Samhain is the time of mystery, magick and most often it is the sabbat/holiday linked to the Occult. For some, like myself, it is the Witches' New Year and October 31st–November 1st is the most potent and powerful 24 hours of the year.

My October is crammed with guest appearances, public speaking engagements, weekly classes, community events and the day and eve of October 31st reserved for family. I have never worked on Halloween, not even when I was a police officer. This day is sacred to me.

Jack-o-lanterns are carved, trick-or-treating and dressing up is a must! Even when growing up, Halloween was taken very seriously by my mother, who would plan elaborate neighborhood block parties that included games, food and plenty of wholesome activities. She and her girlfriends would always dress up and make sure that all of us kids were safe and having a good time.

In our home, we have the biggest feast of the entire year and, as a Pagan who takes "eat, drink and be merry" to heart; we have plenty of feasts throughout the year, but none like Samhain. All the candles in the home are lit, the altar to the ancestors set on October 1st and their names spoken at the table so that they have a formal invitation to join us for the evening and stay, offering their energy and messages until the dawn. For this is a night where the veil drops and the dead walk amongst us.

With the magick of this sabbat, there are numerous animals that are connected to Samhain, such as bats, spiders, werewolves and black cats, to name a few. They each carry with them their own unique attributes and qualities that connect them to this holiday.

Owl is one that often accompanies this most spooky eve. Images of owls watching from bare trees that stand vigil at cemeteries. The hooting of owls is commonly used in haunted houses, spook alleys and useful in creating the ambiance of unknown and things in the dark to fear.

From the time I was about 23–32 years old, owl was my primary spirit animal. I remember vividly when owl came through. I was deep in a time of searching and there was a hooting just outside my bedroom window. It woke me up and I stood by the window and just listened. My heart fluttered and tears came to my eyes. I knew I was shifting from butterfly as my PSA to something else but I just didn't know what; not until this night during the witching hour, when owl was speaking to me.

The next several years were spent soul-searching, researching books, with ideas and taking class after class; anything I could do to gain more knowledge and wisdom – for that is what owl is all about. As a messenger, teacher and guide, owl encourages the individual to seek out that which they do not know – to journey into the depths of one's inner desert; shadow-work and uncover some hidden truths.

Owls are solitary, nocturnal birds that hunt at night feasting mainly upon small mammals. During the day, they rest. One week ago, I was helping my lover of twenty-one years set up a large PA sound system at an outdoor venue in the High Desert of Southern Utah. The venue was surrounded by large red sandstone and in one of the caverns a very large great horned owl sat. Being daytime, the owl typically would have been sleeping but this one seemed curious and she spent most of the day watching us. Sometimes she would preen her feathers and I would wait anxiously below her waiting for one to drop. Eventually she would drop me a feather from her underbelly and this I excitedly received as a gift.

Owls have incredible eyesight despite being farsighted. Unlike their predator cousins, the hawks, owls' eyes are not on the sides of their head but forward-facing, which allows them greater depth perception and to see into the low light of the night. They can rotate their heads about 270 degrees, this is due to them having fourteen neck vertebrae. We humans only have seven.

This great horned owl certainly did not need to give me any of its attention but I was honored. What makes owls so mysterious is their night life which is what connects them to Samhain. As humans, we have been taught to fear the dark.

Growing up I was always told that nothing good ever happened after midnight; that the hours between midnight and 3am were the *witching hours*.

Wikipedia states that, "there is psychological literature suggesting apparitional experiences and sensed presences are most common between the hours of 2am and 4am, corresponding with a 3am peak. In folklore, the witching hour or Devil's hour is the time of night that these supernatural occurrences are most frequently led by witches, demons and ghosts whose peak of power occurs in the dark of night."

Owls are surrounded with rampant superstitions. Just like black cats, they have been hunted and killed for being a witch's familiar or a witch in disguise. In some Native American tribes, owls are messengers of approaching death. "Boreal owl calls were a call from spirits to the Cree People and if you answered back to the owl with a whistle and didn't get a response, it was a sign that your death was imminent."

The Indigenous Aboriginals of Australia believe that owls are the spirits of women and are sacred birds. They have also been linked to witchcraft by the Greeks and Romans, who believed that witches would turn themselves into owls and while in this form they would drain the blood from infants. While other cultures believed that to hear the cry of an owl meant a witch was approaching. The most common theme of superstitions concerning owls is that they are connected with death, which would be why we see frequent images of owls in cemeteries.

With the increase in animal totems, spirit guides and witches' familiars becoming increasingly popular, more and more people are starting to see that animals do contain great mystery and symbolism that can offer insight and direction into our individual lives and earth-based practices.

When you look into the symbolism of owl, you will find descriptive words such as: wise, cunning, vigilant, patient, keen, intuitive, all-knowing, intelligent and all-seeing. The many titles and roles offered to owl include and are not limited to: bringer of wisdom, giver of psychic powers, angel of death, goddess of night, bird of sorcery, messenger of witchcraft, seeker of hidden truths, shadow self, guide of the underworld, messenger from the grave.

Mythology is filled with owl stories from the Norse and Greek to the Celts, just to name three. Not only owls can see into the dark of the night; this very act can teach us that we too can see into the self-created dark of our own souls. Cocking our heads meticulously and finding those truths that we seem to think we have hidden from the world and ultimately ourselves. No matter how you view owls, they are an omen of either good or bad, but that interpretation is completely up to the individual. Animals, like humans, come with polarities – both good and bad aspects, attributes or qualities.

Samhain is the time of year when the dead walk amongst us so it makes sense to honor owl as the mascot and bringer of messages from those in the grave. What better time to set up an ancestor altar and call to the recently deceased and seek advice, counsel and wisdom as we say goodbye to one year and prepare to welcome the new?

REINDEER OF YULE

Reindeer and caribou are species of deer, although some believe reindeer and caribou to be their own unique species found within the family of deer. These majestic creatures are often connected with the Yuletide season. We are all familiar with the song "Rudolph the red nosed reindeer" and the stories that tell us Santa Claus has a sleigh pulled by eight reindeer.

Reindeer can be found in the tundra of the Arctic, northern Europe, Canada and Alaska. There are tundra reindeer and forest reindeer. The tundra species are known for migrating in numbers of close to half million while the forest dwellers remain in the woodlands all year round. Both males and females, referred to as bulls and cows, grow antlers. Bulls use their antlers to fight other bulls for the affections of the nearest cow. While reindeer cows use their antlers to defend against predators. Both shed their antlers, just at different times. Bulls in the late fall/early winter and cows after their winter pregnancy in the spring.

Some interesting facts on reindeer include: their fur, or rather hair, is hollow which allows for insulation and warmth. It's these hollow strands or shafts of hair that give reindeer the white color. They cannot fly like the myths suggest but they are very good swimmers. Reindeer happen to be the only mammal that can see ultraviolet light. Within minutes of being born, a calf can run up to 50mph and travel up to thirty miles a day. Calves do not have spots like their deer cousins. They survive on lichen which is high in protein, vitamins and carbohydrates.

"Reindeer milk is the richest and most nutritious milk produced by any terrestrial mammal. It contains twenty-two percent butterfat and ten percent protein. However they only produce about two cups of milk per day." The Nordic countries make cheese out of reindeer milk.

Speaking of the Norse and Yule, who is the father of the Yuletide season? Why, it's Odin himself! In our home, we do not celebrate holiday season with the traditional *Christmas* symbolism or Santa Claus. The Santa Claus that most people are familiar with, who wears his red velvet suit and has rosy red cheeks, was created by the Coca Cola Company back in the 50's. In our home, we honor our Norse heritage and the God Odin or All-Father of winter with a more Viking flare.

Odin rides upon a majestic eight legged horse named Sleipnir and he too delivers gifts. Odin doesn't come down the chimney like the Coca Cola Santa Claus, instead he leaves toys, trinkets and sweets in boots left out on the eve of December 21st.

https://www.norwegianamerican.com/dont-take-odin-out-of-yule/

In the 1800's, the poem *A Visit from St. Nicholas* described St Nick as being a very tall, gaunt old man with a long white beard, wearing a fur coat and a wide brimmed hat. Well, this description fits one of Odin's favorite disguises – that of the Wanderer. Odin hails from the north and Santa Claus lives at the North Pole. Santa has elves and Odin also has a crew of elves called 'Odin's men' who also, ironically, made gifts for Odin to deliver. My favorite 'aha' similarity is that Santa has two reindeer named 'Donner and Blitzen' which are Germanic words for 'thunder and lightning,' both of which are commanded by Odin and later his son Thor.

Yule is a time for family and friends to feast, drink, give gifts and make merry. Despite the weather and the dangers of a cold winter, coming together as community, pack or tribe created feelings of joy, warmth and light.

Yule occurs on the winter solstice, which is December 21st, and is the longest night and the shortest day of the year. This sabbat honors the rebirth of the Sun and heralds in the beginning of winter. It is one of the oldest winter celebrations known. The entire holiday season (or as the Christians call it; Christmas) is a time of magic, with much focus on rebirth and renewal.

Honoring reindeer makes sense. Their milk is sacred and white as snow. They thrive in the harsh conditions of winter and serve as a beacon, teacher or guide of how to survive. It should be noted that long before the legend of Santa Claus and his eight reindeer, there was a sun goddess whose sleigh was pulled by reindeer. With reindeer being featured on holiday greeting cards, wrapping paper and as iconic figures, we need to remember that all these reindeer with their large antlers are all females – 'cows'. As mentioned earlier, the bulls shed their antlers during fall/winter.

Who is the Deer Mother? She who, according to legend, flew through the longest night? The female reindeer was honored, worshipped and seen as the 'life-giver'. It is said that a herd's entire survival rests upon the leader and that leader is female. Deer Mother or Mother Reindeer has been seen and revered as a spiritual figure of regeneration, motherhood, fertility and rebirth of the Sun, which is the actual theme of Yule! She was honored in Russia, Siberia, Scandinavia, the British Isles and the land bridge of the Bering Strait.

"The Sami, the indigenous people of the Nordic countries honor the Sun Goddess Beaivi whose animal companion is the reindeer. At winter solstice/Yule, warm butter was smeared on doorposts as a sacrifice to Beaivi, so that she could gain strength and fly higher and higher into the sky. Beaivi is often accompanied by her daughter in an enclosure of reindeer antlers and together they returned green and fertility to the land."

There are many 'Deer Mother' goddesses honored by ancient tribes and each goddess is depicted riding a sleigh pulled by reindeer. Talismans, cookies, décor in the shape of reindeer have often been painted, carved and gifted as charms, displayed in homes to protect from evil spirits.

Antlers are seen as magical talismans as well. They are often referred to as the 'Tree of Life' or 'Spiral of Life'. Reindeer antlers represent love, health, longevity and friendship. Antlers are also seen as higher gateways to the other worlds.

Whether Deer Mother is a deity or an actual female deer who flies across the sky in the cold of winter inspiring hope, joy and warmth; she is and has been honored for centuries. In the book *Symbol and Image in Celtic Religious Art*, by Miranda Green, it states: "Early female shamans wore horned headdresses and antlers, for animal symbolism associated with goddesses reaches it apogee with horned female figures, usually adorned with antlers." Reindeer and the Sun are both commonly linked together in Siberian shamanism. The female shamans are most associated with reindeer and are often referred to as Priestesses of the Antlered Ones. You can see why reindeer are the perfect animals to work with and honor in the Yule season.

https://gathervictoria.com/2017/12/15/doe-a-deer-a-female-deer-the-spirit-of-mother-christmas/

BEAR OF IMBOLC

Bears belong to the family Ursidae, which is a fancy name for a group of very large, powerful carnivorous mammals. In all, there are eight species with hundreds of subspecies of bears, with their habitats ranging from North and South America to Europe and Asia. The brown bear alone has over 90 subspecies. It is important to note that not all bears are carnivores – there are six species that are actually omnivores. Bears are often classified as 'carnivores' which means 'dog-like'. This group of carnivores also contains wolves, badgers, raccoons and foxes.

The largest bear is almost a tie between the polar bear (which is classified as a marine animal like a walrus, due to the fact that it spends most of its time at sea) and the Kodiak bear (a subspecies of the brown bear found in Alaska). The sun bear, found in Southeast Asia, is the smallest bear. It may be small in size comparatively to its other bear relatives but the sun bear is quite the site with its foot-long tongue and unique hair pattern that gives it a look of wearing an ancient Egyptian sun necklace.

It's interesting that the giant panda is categorized a bear but the red panda, which resembles more of a raccoon, is in its own family all together. Seems like no one wants to claim it as kin!

With all the subspecies and categories, what stands out is that, even in the animal kingdom, there are more similarities that unite than divide. Something to ponder as we move deeper into the journey of shapeshifting and ultimately remember that we too as mammals have much more in common with our furry brothers and sisters than some choose to see. Would you consider yourself a large bear or a small bear? Or a subspecies? Does placing oneself into a category really matter at all?

Bears have been referred to by many titles and descriptions, from the early Germanic tribes who called them 'brown ones', to the Slavic tribes who called them 'honey-eaters' and the Baltic tribes who called them 'shaggy coats'. The term 'bear' is actually a blanket term, oftentimes misused. For example, the koala bear is not a bear but marsupial. Maybe it is best to refer back to how the early tribes classified animals by their unique physical characteristics. The grizzly bear is, after all, called grizzly because of the grey grizzled hair that grows in its brown fur. Bears are fascinating and each species and subspecies so unique that one could spend weeks and months researching them.

We can lump them all into a category of having some basic physical attributes that are considered similar: large bodies with thick stocky legs, long snouts (with the exception of the spectacled bear) or short faces, small round ears, shaggy hair and paws that feature non-retractable claws and all have a very short tail. But really, that's about it.

The brown bear, or to give it its scientific name, *Ursus* (Latin for bear) *arctos* (Greek for bear), is the second largest bear, next to the polar bear. The brown bear is honored as a national and state animal in several European countries. Its range includes Russia, Central Asia, China, Canada and the US. In North America, the brown bear is referred to as the grizzly bear. The size of each individual subspecies of brown bear really varies upon its location. There are about 200,000 brown bears with Russia housing the largest population, followed by the United States and then Canada. It should be noted that many subspecies of brown bears (California grizzly, Ungava brown bear, Atlas bear and Mexican grizzly) are now extinct, thanks again to the top predator, humans, who hunted them down in the nineteenth and early twentieth century's.

A male brown bear weighs about 300-900 pounds with the females weighing about 300-800 pounds with an average life span of fifteen to twenty-five years. Brown bears have a very distinct shoulder hump unlike the American black bear and polar bear. Brown bears are omnivores and eat just about anything, making them very large scavengers and frequent visitors of national parks and campground, dining on garbage and food not properly stored.

In Alaska, Washington and Canada they thrive on salmon, as portrayed in the Disney cartoon movie *Brother Bear*, when Koda and Kenai make their way to the salmon run.

In this scene, the salmon run is a festival gathering of brown bears all different shades and sizes, chowing down on salmon. Compared to actual footage of brown bears catching salmon, there is an obvious camaraderie amongst the bears in the movie, with the common goal being to catch as many salmon as possible; there are however occasional fights and disputes over the best fishing spots. Unlike the cartoon that is one big family sing along, brown bears are typically solitary, unless it is a mother and her cubs.

They are not pack animals and only seek out other bears during mating season and to hunt salmon. A female bear does not begin mating until she is between the ages of four to six years old. The mating season takes place between May-July. During this time, she will mate will multiple males. In the fall, the female enters her den for a hibernation period and about eight weeks later, the cubs are born. Tiny and hairless, weighing less than a pound, a female bear will have anywhere from one to three cubs. Like the polar bear, the male brown bear plays no part in parenting and raising the cubs. They are actually one of the greatest threats to young cubs.

Despite how they are often portrayed in cinema, bears are not ferocious. While they are not pack animals, they are very aware of other bears in their territory and typically will respect each other. There is a natural hierarchy dependent upon age, size and temperament. When startled or protecting cubs, they may charge and attack, but brown bears interact with a threat in their own unique ways, unlike the black bear subspecies that often flee instead of defend, retreating into a tree. Brown bears are more likely to stay on the ground and face the threat.

In 1994, three cave explorers made a life-changing discovery in the south of France when they located a cave that was about 400 meters long with many chambers. The floors were covered with skulls and bones of cave bears and two wolves. On the walls of the cave was primitive art in shades of red and black. The cave paintings depict animals, from lions and mammoths to rhinoceroses and bears, just to name a few. Most of these images have been dated back to 30,000 years ago. In this cave, there are also scratch marks made by cave bears, some human footprints and an image of the lower body of a woman next to a bison. What a remarkable experience it must have been to step into that cave and see the painted walls! I can't imagine.

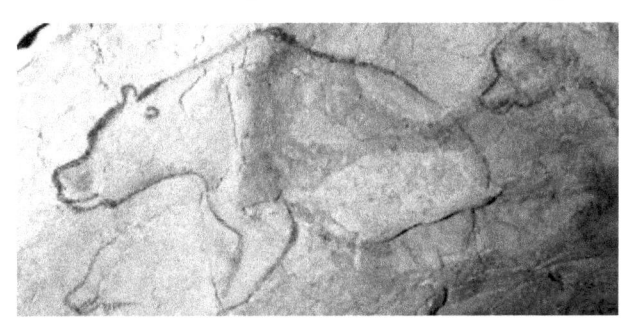

Bears have been revered and worshipped by many different cultures and tribes. From the ancient Slavic people to Finnish, Pyrenees, Celts and the Ainu people of Japan. Archaeologists have found remains of bears carefully arranged in what appear to be ceremonial burials. The Finns (a polytheistic indigenous Scandinavian people) believed that bears came from the constellation Ursa Major. Bears are so respected in Finland that they are not allowed to be hunted and even the word 'bear' is too sacred to use, so the Finnish people have over 1,000 different nicknames for bears.

Archaeologists have found a bear figure in Finland dating back to 5100 BC. In eastern Finland, the bear was believed to be the ancestor of the clan as many believed bears shared similar characteristics with humans from their ability to stand on their hind legs making them the size of a grown man, their paws resemble human hands complete with five fingers and

THE WHEEL OF THE YEAR

they had qualities that were admired by these early hunters and gatherers.

The Celts honored Artio, a bear goddess of fertility, transformation, abundance, strength, the wild, and the spring. She is depicted as a mother bear or oftentimes a woman wearing a bear hide. She too came down to Earth from the skies. Many people believe that the bear is the oldest of the European deities, based on the bear skulls and bones found all over in sacred caves and burial sites throughout Europe. Judith Shaw writes that, "Further evidence of Artio's ancient origins is found in the first written sentence from the *old Europe script* invented around 6,000 years ago, long before the Celts arrived. It reads '*The Bear Goddess and the Bird Goddess are the Bear Goddess indeed.*'"

In 1832, a statue was found in a garden in Switzerland. It is of a bear on all fours being fed by a woman seated on a chair, a tree is behind the bear's hind leg. On the statue is an inscription which reads: "To the Goddess Artio." The ancestors of the Celts came from what we know today to be Germany, Austria and Switzerland, they brought the worship of their gods and goddesses with them. The Celtic tribe the Helvetii migrated from Bavaria to Switzerland and were known for worshipping Artio as the "she-bear." Artio has been compared to the Goddess Elen of the Ways for her wild goddess aspect and embodiment of Nature in all its glory. She is beloved as a protector and great mother goddess who sees all, who follows her as her cubs and she will guide them to a deeper knowledge and powerful transformation. Artio was believed to be a goddess of plenty, prosperity and the harvest. Most depictions show her to have lots of baskets filled with fruits and nuts and surrounded by many animals of the forest.

Bear magic and worship has been seen and embraced in many main characters in ancient myths and legends from King Arthur to the All Father Odin in Norse mythology. Why bears? Even the Celtic Goddess Brigid or by her other name, St Birgitta, is oftentimes seen as a bear; the Great Bear Mother, for in the winter she rests and in the spring she is reborn. The Great Bear Mother is like other mother goddesses.... Wise, patient, teaching, loving, nurturing and fiercely protective of her young.

In the winter when a female bear hibernates, it appears that she is half dead, for her heartbeat slows and her breathing is barely noticeable. Yet in the spring, this same bear that was thought to be near death awakens from her slumber with new life; cubs, and it is as if the Great Bear Mother has once again saved everyone from the death of winter and quickens hope for a new spring. Much like Brigid does at her festival day of February 1st, when the earth begins to quicken and stir with new life. Brigid, like the Great Bear, is the great mother and midwife who ignites the spark of new life into all who embrace her.

As I write this, we are in the midst of winter, a recent snow storm has covered the earth with a blanket of white. A reminder to slow down and spend some conscious time doing inner workings or hibernating from the hustle and bustle of the everyday chaos. We are also in the end of January – the season of Imbolc. When the Great Mother Bear begins to quicken from her winter slumber and slowly awaken from her deep winter's sleep to the arrival of spring. New life beginning to stir within and without, for all things are connected. As above so below.

Imbolc is based upon the Celtic tradition of honoring the halfway or midpoint between the winter solstice and the spring equinox. A cross quarter event if often referred to as Bear Day by the early Europeans. It typically is celebrated from February 1st to the 2nd. A magickal time of year when the Sun gets a bit brighter, days lengthen and the plants begin to quicken and awaken under the ground in preparation for spring flowers.

Gail Faith Edwards says; "It is time, now, to reclaim the potent friendship and reverence of the Bear Mother of our ancestors. Time to realize that we too can be fierce beyond measure. We too can be a healing blessing for our community. Bear Mother is more than an ally and an inspiration. She is a powerful guardian spirit. With all that we are presently facing, in national and world politics, global changes and personal survival challenges, we need her. We need to become her, as our ancestors did. We need to act with her agency. Get your claws ready, your thick protective coat wrapped snugly around your shoulders, do not fear to bare your teeth. Today honor Bear Mother. Feel her awakening in all her glory, within us."

HARE OF OSTARA

Hares, although related to rabbits, making them cousins; are actually larger than rabbits. They have rather pronounced ears and longer hind legs. They typically have black tipped ears and, while rabbits' fur stays the same color all year long, a hare goes from brown to white in the winter. Baby hares are born fully furred, eyes open and hopping around; they are able to survive on their own within hours of being born. Baby rabbits are helplessly blind, hairless and rely upon their mothers up until 6-8 weeks old. Most rabbits live in family groups, while hares are solitary. Rabbits also burrow in the ground and hares live on the surface. It should be noted that hares and rabbits, although related and considered to be in the same family, do not mate with each other; as they are genetically incompatible. Hares eat hardier foods such as bark, twigs and thick plant shoots. Rabbits eat grasses, soft stems and vegetables.

There is a fondness and appreciation amongst the Pagan community when it comes to the hare. Many different pantheons center on myth and legend, with the hare being one of the animals that possesses great medicine and magick.

In the fable, *The Tortoise and the Hare*, the hare brags and boasts about how fast he is, poking fun at all the other animals, but especially the tortoise. The tortoise however proclaims that, while the hare may be fast, the tortoise could still beat him in a race. So they race! The hare being ever so arrogant, he took off with great speed, while the tortoise kept to his slow and steady pace. The hare could barely see the tortoise behind him, so he stopped for a bit to snack and play. Then, deciding he obviously was going to win with miles between him and the tortoise, he lay down and took a nice long nap. All the while, the tortoise kept going, moving with step by step precision. It took some time, but the tortoise went right past the sleeping hare, who had no idea he had napped as long as he had, until he woke up and realized the tortoise was crossing the finish line.

What's the moral of the story? We all know it to be: 'slow and steady wins the race.' Dave Ramsey states that "we live in a culture full of hares; but the tortoise always wins." The question to ask oneself is: are you a tortoise or a hare? And why?

While Aesop's fable depicts the hare as being egotistical and arrogant, in other myths, legends and pantheons the hare is seen quite differently. For example, to the Algonquin tribe of eastern Canada, the Great Hare known as Michabo is supreme deity and creator of the human race. A shapeshifter or shape-changer, Michabo was the grandson of the Moon. Son of his father; the west wind and mother; the dawn. Michabo is creator of religious rites, dreams and writing. Michabo, also known as Mishàbòz, Michabou, Michabous, Michaboo, Mishabo, Michebo, Messou, Missabos, Misabos, Misabooz, Missiwabun and Messon, is derived from *missi,* which means great, and *wabos* meaning rabbit.

Even the Egyptians look to hare as a supreme creator and goddess known as Unut, Wenet or Wenenut – the female partner of the god Weneu, also a hare god. Both are depicted as having the head of a hare. Wenet symbolized renewal of the land, fertility and protection. Some scholars believe that both god and goddess were connected with the Underworld as sacred guards.

The belief of hares and rabbits as being supreme beings that are connected to the world below stems from their ability to go within the earth into their burrows whenever they wanted.

Hares are honored as androgynous beings that shift between both genders. Depending on which pantheon, hares will be interchangeable in their yin/yang attributes and characteristics.

In male form, the hare is seen as wild, arrogant, promiscuous and a trickster, similar the coyote or the god Loki. While in female form, the hare is seen as gentle, sensitive and connected with the Moon. Lunar symbolism is embraced in just about every pantheon. This is because for centuries, the hare has been connected with the Moon. One just needs to look up and see the long ears and body of the hare. It is believed that if one sees the hare on the Moon, good fortune and abundance would follow.

The hare is also associated with the Goddess of Spring; *Eostre,* whose festival day; Ostara, happens to coincide with the first day of spring or the spring equinox, around March 21st. While there is no concrete evidence which pantheon this flower goddess is from, there are plenty of Pagan, Wiccan and Neopagan authors who agree that she is the inspiration for the holiday Easter. Certainly her name has similar spelling and pronunciations. It should be noted that the Christian holiday of Easter has a different date each year and that date is determined by the Moon. The holiday is set to happen on the first Sunday after the full moon following the spring equinox.

March is the midpoint of the hare's breeding season. Males go to great lengths and extremes to attract the attention of the females. However, with this excited and unpredictable behavior, some females don't have much patience. While the male is putting on quite the show with his leaping, jumping and chasing, eventually the female gives him a hard smack and then they begin to box. Kicking at each other with their large hind legs and literally boxing each other with their front paws. It's quite the mating match.

One year in my community, at our annual Ostara spring equinox, I decided to have the ritual be a mad hatter's tea party style and invoked the essence of the Mad March Hare. I was unprepared for what would happen. Two days after our event, my husband told me to come and look outside.

We literally had nine white rabbits running around our yard! This is not a natural phenomenon as white rabbits are domesticated and do not run wild here in the High Desert. But sure enough, we had nine white rabbits. It was all very *Alice in Wonderland*.

We came to find out that our neighbor had a friend who had acquired the white rabbits in a divorce outcome and had decided to just let them loose. Our yard happens to be the more inviting and enticing yard so they came through the fence. It took us a few weeks to relocate them to better homes. The moral we learned is; to be careful when you call in the madness of the March Hare, as the energies can be very unforeseeable.

> "You might just as well say,"
> said the March Hare,
> "that 'I like what I get' is the same as 'I get what I like!'"

AND:
"I'm not strange, weird, off, nor crazy.
My reality is just different from yours."

Lewis Carroll

When you look at an image of or see a hare in its natural habitat, there are physical characteristics that stand out. The long ears, big eyes and long hind legs with large feet. All these highlight the animal's senses. Hares have an excellent sense of smell and superb hearing. These abilities allow them to know when a predator is nearby. They can hop up to ten feet and can reach running speeds of 35 to 40mph. Hares are also excellent swimmers.

Again, we have polarity magick working and we know that polarity is vital for growth and creating balance. Hares are both good and bad; just like most people contain both good and bad traits. The hare teaches us to be clever, to be quick, that it's okay to be secretive, mysterious, sexual and a little bit mad.

It's both interesting and sad, looking back on legends and myths, how the deities shapeshifted into hares in a way that was positive and admirable. Shapeshifting seemed to be common practice amongst the gods and goddesses of old. The hare being another depiction of the Great Goddess/Divine Feminine herself. Yet, when Christianity came into play, things changed and this once embraced form of deity-shifting with hares became tainted and used as a weapon in the witch hunts of Scotland and England when it was believed that witches would often shift into hares, crows, ravens and dogs as well as black cats.

One witch in particular even confessed to shifting into a hare. This witch in Scotland now infamously known as the 'Queen of Witches' was Isobel Gowdie. Isobel gave a very detailed confession in which she admitted to being able to shift into the form of many animals, along with her coven sisters; one such animal being the hare. In her confession she stated: "When we go into hare-shape we say: I shall go into a hare, with sorrow and sigh, and meikle care. And I shall go in the Devil's name, aye while I come home again."

When I began my journey into my ancestry I was excited to find out that one of my ancestors was Sir Walter Scott, who wrote the book *Demonology and Witchcraft* – a compilation of letters that he wrote to his son-in-law as an effort to discuss in a more informal analytical manner the witch hunts and hysteria and prove that the prosecutions were political and directed against heretics.

In one passage he states: "Metamorphoses were, according to Isobel, very common among them, and the forms of crows, cats, hares and other animals, were on such occasions assumed." In her very detailed testimony, she tells of an incident when in hare form (her most favored animal form). She was sent on an errand by the Devil to Auldearn with a message to her neighbors when she came across Peter Papley who had his hounds with him. The dogs quickly ran after the hare. Isobel, as hare, ran as fast as she could to escape the dogs; in her efforts to not get eaten, she was able to retreat back into her house where she hid behind a chest of drawers and had just enough time to recite the incantation of "Hare, hare, God send thee care! I am in a hare's likeness now; but I shall be a woman even now – Hare, hare, God send thee care!" Upon which, the enchantment was released and she stood as a woman once more and quickly excused the dogs from her home.

BUTTERFLIES OF BELTANE

Nothing quite says spring like butterflies. The first to usually arrive in our area is the cabbage white followed by the mourning cloak. Butterflies are insects. You may wonder why I am including butterflies under the blanket term 'animals'; remember that, as an animist, I view all things of Nature as whole, divine, sentient and vibrating with their own souls. Butterflies can show up as someone's PSA, totem of a tribe and messenger, teacher or guide.

For quite a while, the swallowtail butterfly was my PSA. In fact, when my lover and I became engaged, we saw tiger swallowtails every day of our engagement. We welcomed them as a sign and symbol that our love was new, exciting and blessed. Even on our wedding day, we were blessed with not just one but two tiger swallowtails.

As a PSA, I honored and welcomed butterfly as messenger and guide for close to seven years. My right shoulder even has a tattoo of one. So, yes! Butterflies can be sacred teachers, just like wasps, praying mantis and any other insect.

There are close to 20,000 species of butterflies. Most of these bright and colorful, fairy-like insects really only live for a few weeks. They use their feet to taste and their day to day activities include mating and eating.

Beltane falls on May 1st and is a cross quarter day that celebrates the approaching summer. Beltane on the Wheel of the Year calendar sits right in the middle of the spring equinox/Ostara and summer solstice/Litha. In Gaelic, the word means 'bright fire'. Typical celebrations consist of frolicking, making merry and feasting – very similar to the life of a butterfly – which is why I picked butterfly.

Think if you will of two large bonfires and in the middle is a pathway that the cattle would be walked on. The fires were kept hot as to burn up any parasites and bless the cattle before putting them out to pasture. Fire is both purifying and healing.

In Ireland, there are a few different superstitions surrounding butterflies. For example, if you see a yellow one then success will follow. If you see brown or black butterflies then something is going to come along and create an inconvenience. A white butterfly could very well be the soul of a deceased child. To kill a butterfly will bring about bad luck. In other stories, butterflies are associated with the fire gods, the deana-dhe which means 'magical flame'.

While bonfires are the focal point for Beltane, another activity that is also common is dancing around the maypole, which symbolizes a fertility rite – the pole representing the masculine and the ribbons the feminine. Planting a garden is also another way to increase magic in the land. When we plant gardens, we attract butterflies which bring with them Fae energy. Plants love Fae energy!

Beltane is deeply connected to the mystery of the Fae. Beltane, like Samhain, is believed to be the time when the veil between the living and the Fae is dropped. Beltane and Samhain are directly across from each other on the Wheel of the Year, so they are natural mirrors of each other.

Because of the miraculous metamorphosis that butterflies go through in their brief lifespan, they are the cover model for all things transformational. If you see butterflies in your life, often take inventory of the areas in your life that you need to change or ways in which you are ready to transform. After all, change is the only constant in life. Why not embrace it with grace?

Butterflies symbolize hope, change, joy, play and endurance. They are social beings, which classifies them as symbols or sigils of friendship, relationships and community. Butterflies remind me to be more joyful and take life less seriously – to dance and play more. Have you visited a costume shop and put on butterfly or fairy wings? That inner child comes out to play when wearing wings. Beltane is such a lively sabbat commonly associated with dressing up and playing out different roles, being mischievous, daring and breaking free from the social norms.

Even Christianity has embraced the butterfly as a symbol of hope and the spirit world. Butterflies in many countries are considered other-worldly beings or spirits who have crossed over; or spirits that are watching over.

As a mirror, butterflies show us that we all move through life in stages and that is okay! I love the quote by Rupi Kaur: "You do not just wake up and become a butterfly. Growth is a process." Another great quote from her book, *The Little Prince*, is: "Well, I must endure the presence of a few caterpillars if I wish to become acquainted with the butterflies."

When you dance the dance of Beltane with butterflies as your inspiration, you can create a sabbat of play, merriment and vigor. So put on those wings and activate your lustful maiden and knight. Make love and make magick.

HUMMINGBIRD OF LITHA

Hummingbirds are tiny beings that can fly backwards, they have no sense of smell and their little wings beat so fast they sound as if they are buzzing – quite literally humming. Hummingbirds are the smallest birds and they weigh less a nickel. Tiny humming bits of magick.

Energetically, to see a hummingbird is to activate joy, healing and good luck. I have had numerous clients who have had a loved one pass away and then they started seeing hummingbirds everywhere. Could these tiny birds be the souls of beloveds who have crossed over? Well butterflies are linked to that same belief in many cultures, so it's not impossible.

Summer is a time of full bloom, the heat of the Sun is at its peak and in my garden it is a rare treat to see Hummingbirds – due mostly to the fact that we live way out in the valley and our yard is the only one in miles to have any flowers for the hummingbirds to feed on. But they do pay a visit. Just last week, when I was weeding the flowerbed beside our labyrinth, I heard a buzzing and, expecting to see a bumblebee, I was quite pleased to see a hummingbird suspended in front of me just looking at me as its wings hummed. That brief moment was enough to inspire me to connect with hummingbird for our upcoming Litha or summer solstice sabbat.

The act of zipping up to one's face and staring is quite common for hummingbirds, which are incredibly intelligent and inquisitive. These birds are very curious. There are many reasons a hummingbird may hover and stare you down. Maybe they are sizing you up as a threat or they want food. The color red attracts them, which is why most hummingbird feeders are red in color. When they stop and take notice of you, they give you an opportunity to stop and take notice of them. Maybe they are offering some inspiration or encouragement?

Hummingbirds are so fast and their entire life is spent searching and consuming food. Because of their rapid metabolism they must eat every ten minutes. Which means their daily average consists of one to two thousand flowers a day. Not only do they need to consume ample amounts but they have incredible memories and they know which hot spots to frequent.

Like ravens, hummingbirds are highly intelligent and they can and do remember faces. If you want to attract hummingbirds into your yard, be diligent. Fill their feeders around the same time of each feeding day and they will wait patiently. They will also become familiar with one's voice and one's day to day patterns in the yard. So, as you study them, rest assured they are studying you.

Summer solstice occurs right around June 21st and it marks the peak of summer. It is the longest day of the year – a fertility sabbat and outdoor celebration as all things experience an increase in energy and an excitement to do more things outdoors.

This past summer solstice, I took a pilgrimage to the home of my High Priestess Zsuzsanna Budapest, for the first sabbat in our coven since COVID-19. It was a lovely event filled with the buzzing and humming of happy chatter as guests hugged and shared stories of what their past year was like and how they had made the best of the global pandemic situation. Seeing everyone so happy and full of vigor is what summer should be like and is intended to be like by most.

Summer is a time of play and, much like the hummingbird, a time of flitting from one place to another in a much faster pace than, say, the butterfly. Hummingbirds are quick! So quick they average up to 30mph; even more when trying to entice a mate. Between all the events, hikes, lake visits, travels, barbecues and more, summer always seems to go by so quickly. Just like a hummingbird; in the blink of an eye; it's gone!

There are over 300 species of hummingbirds. Females are the nest builders and lay two eggs which, on average, are about the size of peas. The male is not involved in the raising of the young, at three weeks; he will leave their tiny nest. Hummingbirds are migrating birds and have been known to travel up to 23 miles in one day. Stopping, of course, every ten minutes to feast.

Hummingbirds do sleep and they do rest. They are not highly social and prefer a more solitary life. They, like most animals, are being affected by the change in our climate which has made their migratory patterns difficult. Believe it or not, the praying mantis is a major predator to the hummingbird, as they will wait patiently at the feeders and then attack.

Litha is a time of bonfires, celebrating the heat of the Sun and the abundance of life all around. Just about every flower is at full bloom which means, if they are pink, red or purple, then hummingbirds will be out and about buzzing around. Like Beltane, Litha is very focused on Fae energy with some practitioners of the craft calling on the Fae to enchant and enhance their Litha festivities.

Have you ever heard stories or seen images of fairies riding on hummingbirds? Children, by their very inquisitive nature, often refer to hummingbirds as fairies. Who is to say? After all, hummingbirds do move incredibly fast and are very whimsical. Maybe, just maybe, they are a bit Fae?

EAGLE OF LUGHNASADH

Lughnasadh marks the first of the three harvest seasonal sabbats. It's a time when summer magick has hit fruition and gardens are in full production, farmers' markets are thriving and with synchronicity people have begun to gather, bottle and prepare foods for the upcoming winter months. Having a garden is an act of rebellion and magick daily. It is harnessing the power of creation and seeing transformation happen right before your eyes. To stick a seed into the ground in the early spring, water, tend and watch it grow, bloom and produce bounty is the purest form of magick! I love the first harvest, mostly because it means an end to the heat of summer. Not that I loathe summer but in the desert the heat can be overwhelming and make working in the garden a hot, sweaty and uncomfortable situation.

With Lughnasadh, there is that first taste of bliss as you pick that ripe and ready tomato that you have been eyeing with eagerness. I love a good sun-ripened tomato fresh off the vine. That is something worthy of celebrating. This time of year, we also see an abundance of eagles flying up above. I am so thankful every day for having so much wildlife around me.

Eagle represents solar energy and freedom. In 1782, the eagle became a national symbol for the United States. Eagles have served as Divine Chief and leader of strength, victory and seeing things from a higher perspective. They are birds that represent honor and believing in one's self and one's capabilities.

Eagles have been honored by the early Native American tribes as sources of great resilience and renewed vigor for life. Native Elders use eagle feathers in their ceremonies, prayers and as a way to connect through visions with the Great Spirit or Realm of the Spirits.

They were also seen as sacred birds of power and courage by the Romans. The God Jupiter used the eagle as one of his symbols. Even Moses from the Bible speaks of eagles as having spiritual power. To the Celts, the eagle was an animal that represented authority, focus, security and leadership.

Anytime a large bird, especially a major predator, shows up I often ask myself, "what is going on in my life that would benefit from a new perspective?" Eagles are the large ruler of the skies. They are stunning to see in flight and magnificent to watch tear into their prey. They have excellent vision and they can spot prey up to 3.2 km away. Their talons can grasp up to ten times stronger than humans. Makes you rethink that "get a grip" phrase.

A group of eagles is referred to as a convocation. So with the first harvest being a time when the Sun is at its highest and the plants are all vibrating on that life source, gather you convocation and have a feast, make merry and be sure to share your homegrown goodies.

Eagles are often linked to the namesake of this sabbat Lugh. Myth tells us that Lugh was dealt a death blow and let out a mighty scream and transformed himself into an eagle who took flight quickly and took refuge at the top of an oak tree. Even in death, Lugh was powerful. Eagle represented rebirth and transformation. Both Lugh and eagle teach us flexibility and mastery of skills. "Lugh teaches us to set our aims high and not to be attached to an outcome as the most divine gifts come in the most unexpected ways and from the most unexpected places."

In Druid rites honoring this sabbat, eagle is sky father and invoked when calling in the directional elements of the east. Eagle is Lord of the Winds. When you see an eagle in the sky, what feelings surface? What inspires you about eagle? How does eagle demand you take notice?

SALMON OF MABON

Mabon represents the second harvest sabbat. It is a time of reflection of where you have come, what seeds you planted, harvested and preserved. In our home it is Thanksgiving. Our garden is rampant with edible goodness and we have plenty to share, so a feast and gratitude for all that we have accomplished is fitting.

For me Mabon is reflection. Honoring ancestry and spending time looking back at what our ancestors did to prepare for the upcoming winter. What did they do to ensure their survival? At this Harvest winter is literally knocking on the door and it is a time of hard work, perseverance and making sure all is gathered, bottled and preserved from the garden so nothing is wasted.

Salmon are incredible! They are the epitome of perseverance and hard work. For me, they represent deep dedication and their goal is survival. Just like our ancestors, who worked hard in their land to ensure an abundant season in order for their community/clan to survive, they persevered.

In North America, there are six species of salmon (Salmo salar – literally meaning to leap) five come from the Pacific and one from the Atlantic; which is the largest of the Salmon. Each species of salmon, while similar as they are all fish, are actually very different.

For example, the Chinook is the largest; with a black mouth and black gums. While the coho has a black mouth with white gums. The sockeye has a white mouth and white gums. Every species of salmon is distinct, has their own strengths and even their own taste, although I will have to trust what others say on that, as I am vegan.

What unites the salmon fish is that they are all a species of ray-finned fish in the family of salmonidae. There are other fish in this large family as well, including the trout. Salmon hatch in fresh water, migrate to the ocean, then return back to fresh water to reproduce or spawn.

This instinctual desire or rather drive to return to the exact spot where they hatched is referred to as the Great Salmon Migration. Salmon will often travel up to 200 miles up-river to return to the very spot where they hatched to mate, spawn and then die. Why travel back to their birthplace just to die? Talk about bringing things full circle?!

How do they know their way home? Some researchers believe that salmon use microscopic crystals of magnetite in their tissue as a map and compass to navigate the Earth's magnetic field. These magnetic pulses have been found to alter orientation behavior not only in salmon but mole rats, bats, birds, sea turtles and lobsters. Chemical magnetoreception is another theory, whereby biochemical reactions produce an effective navigation tool.

THE WHEEL OF THE YEAR

When salmon are in fresh water, they imprint with the chemical makeup of the water. When they reach salt water, they rely upon geomagnetic cues. They remember the longitude and latitude. They rely upon the chemical signals and magnetic field to help them know which route to take back home. Even after so much time has passed, they have a *knowing*.

Do the salmon, which migrate along the same route that their ancestors have done for hundreds of years, experience a knowing? Do they feel their ancestors guiding them? While I am sure scientists may argue with me, I firmly believe that our ancestors are guiding us in so many ways and for so many reasons.

When we actively engage in the Wheel of the Year, we are doing so in part to connect with the land, the elements and our ancestors. The quest to uncover bloodlines and connect with ancestors is not new. In 2019, over 26 million people have offered up their DNA for a glimpse into the past and discover who they came from and where they came from. While genealogy was once reserved for the wealthy to help establish inheritance, in the 1970's there was a surge to discover more than just one's grandparents but one's family history. While for some, genealogy is just a hobby, others have made it a profession. You can hire an expert to research and locate your genealogical history or you can utilize many free online websites that can do a very similar job.

In winter of 2020, I ordered a DNA kit and really lost track of time once I received my results. Hours and hours were spent diving through my maternal bloodline and my paternal bloodline. During my research, I uncovered many ancestors who were of royal blood and even found tombstones, maps of their birthplaces and so much more. It is easy to get lost in the past and feel somehow connected to these ancestors. Through my devotion to uncovering where my family came from and learning about which family member was the first to reach the United States, I felt a deep and profound longing to go on a pilgrimage once again to retrace the steps of my actual ancestors.

The dictionary defines pilgrimage as: "1: a journey of a pilgrim especially to a shrine or sacred place. 2: the course of life on Earth." In November of 2018, my lover and I made an intentional pilgrimage to England and Scotland to retrace the steps of our ancestors. My lover had done much more research than me (thanks to the genealogy work done by his grandmother and mother) and he had a clear idea of where in England we were headed. We ended up in Preston, a city in Lancashire, northern England. What an incredible feeling to walk around a town that his ancestors lived in, who walked the same streets we were now on. My family line took me to Scotland. The incredible feeling of being home was oftentimes so powerful I would have to pause and take deep breaths. There is something ancient in the land and you can feel it in a sacred pilgrimage…. That magic of connection.

Even on our ancestral pilgrimage, things just happened that were synchronistic and simply too profound to ignore. We came home after two weeks and began planning our next one. Now with our DNA results and even more information on our ancestral line, we have more knowledge and more motivation to go back and dive deeper into the past of our bloodlines. In a way, we are salmon people seeking more, wanting a journey to connect us to the past so that we can amplify the present.

CHAPTER SEVEN

Collection of Sabbat Ceremonies

SAMHAIN AND OWL CEREMONY

Creating an Intention
For this ceremony, we will be calling owl for wisdom as messenger between the realm of the living and the dead. Setting up an ancestral altar is a great way of stepping into the intentional celebrating of this sabbat. Include nicely framed pictures of your ancestors and/or recently deceased that you wish to invite and seek counsel from.

Altar Set Up
Create your focal point for this ceremony using altar cloths the colors of black, white, silver, gold and orange.

To represent the east you can use feathers; south orange; black candles, west a cauldron; and north skulls or bones.

In the center of your altar have an owl figurine, painting or even stuffed animal. Finding an owl statue should not be hard this time of year. A candle dedicated to owl is fitting and should be placed beside or in front of the owl figurine.

Lastly, you will need a picture or object of the ancestor or recently departed that you wish to connect with (yes, this can be a pet that has recently crossed over the rainbow bridge).

One plate, one chalice and libations (cake and ale).

Breathing into Ceremony Space

Now that your space is set up and your intention known, take some time to energetically connect with your physical and spiritual realms.

If you are offering this ceremony to a group, beginning with meditation is a great way of honoring each other and allowing each other an opportunity to shift in to the magick of being present.

> Begin by closing your eyes and focusing on your breath.
> Take a nice deep, cleansing inhale and deep, cleansing exhale.
> Repeat this up to five times.
> Give yourself permission to physically relax and clear your mind.
> Send down your energetic roots and connect with the ground.
> Send up your energetic branches and connect with above.
> Feel the energy as it moves around you.
> Caressing you. Inviting you to take notice.
> This is a time of intense energetic shifts as the veil between the living and the dead has dropped and the spirits of the Underworld walk amongst us here in the living.
> Feel as they too begin to connect with this space, this here and this now.
> When you feel anchored and held by the energy and magick of being present, open your eyes.

Clearing the Space

Smudge and water blessing are both appropriate for clearing your ritual space. Again, I prefer to use herbs in season and do loose incense blends.

This time of year, however, the Earth has already begun her slumber, so oftentimes I will burn frankincense or myrrh gum in the cauldron on the south of the altar.

Water blessing is typically done with moon water with a pinch of pink Himalayan salt.

Creating the Container

Remember to honor your tradition and cast your circle in your own way – calling, summoning or inviting the directional elements and archetypes.

When working with animals in casting, you can create a more intense focus by inviting animals that are local to your area that are thriving at this time of year. For example, in my area at this ritual I would sing a song of welcome to the ravens of the east, spiders of the south, scorpions of the west and skunks of the north – as at this time of year, these animals are seen often.

When we connect with the elements and animals in our own environment we deepen the magick.

Welcome Summoning to Owl

On this the Eve of All Hallows'/Samhain
I light this candle and call to Great Owl of Wisdom.
Keeper of insight and knowledge.
Messenger between the realms of living and dead.
I call to owl and ask that you extend an invitation with your hooting to

(say the name of your ancestor/recently deceased, out loud),

so they may they hear your sacred call and join me this night.
I call to owl, who is regal with fierce intellect.
Help me to open my eyes that I may see.
Help me to open my ears that I may hear.
Help me to open my heart that I may feel and absorb the messages from beyond.
I call to owl on this most sacred night when the veil has dropped.
I call to owl and ask you to lead

(say the name of your ancestor/recently deceased, out loud)

to this space, this night, this here and this now.
Hail and welcome.

Body of Ceremony

Light the owl candle. Pour libations into the chalice and place upon plate. Sit before your altar and take some time within the quiet to really connect.

Think of your dearly departed/ancestor and welcome them to sit with you and know that the libations you have poured and placed are for them. Invite owl to circle above your space and perch when ready.

This ceremony is quiet and typically dark, with all but the one candle, so take some time to adjust to this space. This liminal realm where all things are possible.

When you feel comfortable, lie down or stay seated.

Ceremonial Meditation Connection

Bring your awareness once more onto your breath

(move through your inhale and exhale to the count of four and repeat at least five times).

Here in this space of liminal you are relaxed and open to receiving messages from the beyond,

for the beyond is now all around.

See, in your mind's eye or inner sight, your ancestor or dearly departed sitting with you.

Feel as wings of owl take flight and create a gentle breeze.

Invite owl to sit or perch beside you as well.

With the herald of death, and your visitor beside you, take some time and connect.

Ask them questions. Speak to them as if they are really there – for they are.

What insight of wisdom do they have for you as you prepare to say goodbye to this year and begin to welcome in the new? Open your eyes.

Journal Prompt

You may want to write down the messages you have received before moving on.

Offer Gratitude

Now that you have spent some time with owl and your dearly departed; snuff, pinch or blow out the owl candle. Offer thanks to owl and the directions in your own way and tradition.

> **• Leave a plate of libations out for any other ancestors and spirits who wish to visit you •**

YULE AND REINDEER CEREMONY

Intention

This time of the year is a time to honor the mother energies of fertility, abundance and rebirth – for we all come from a mother.

It is also a time for birth and celebrating the rebirth of the Sun, as the days begin to grow longer and spring is approaching.

Altar Set Up

To create the flow and intention for this ceremony, begin with altar cloth(s) that are green, red, white, gold, silver. Or fur pelts, if you have any.

Honor each direction on the altar with items that represent each element in a seasonal manner. For example, in the east – holly berries; south – red candles; green – candles; west – cauldron filled with snow or ice chips; north – Yule log.

In the center of the altar is where you can place antler sheds, a reindeer figure or picture. Please have at least one candle set aside for the Reindeer-Mother.

Any evergreen boughs are ideal for adding color and life to the altar.

Optional
Yule log, gifts for a gift exchange, liquid libation for toasting ritual.

Clear your Space
In your own way and own tradition, smudge and water-bless your space.

This time of year, I prefer to use loose incense of frankincense, myrrh and rosemary for remembrance.

Anchor into the Space with Meditative Breath Work

> Close your eyes and breathe into the space and your intention. Create a rhythm of inhales and exhales, breathing in the count of four and out to the count of four.
>
> (repeat at least five times)
>
> Instead of sending your roots down and branches up, see yourself sitting upon the frozen snow-covered ground of winter. Feel the calm, the quiet. Sit in quiet for a few moments and just feel winter.

When you feel the calm and quiet, open your eyes.

Create the Container
In your own way and honoring your own tradition, call to the directional elements and animal archetypes.

It is always best to honor those animals that are in your local area. Or you can focus on the animals of the season.

Call of Summoning to Reindeer-Mother

Here in hallowed, sanctioned space we call to Reindeer-Mother.
She whose antlers reach into the beyond as tethers to the other worlds.
She who is calm, serene and offers a gentle love.
We call to Reindeer-Mother.
Fill this hearth and home with warmth that all may survive this winter that is upon us.
Offer us your protection.
We call to Reindeer-Mother.
She who is life giving, life sustaining. She who is milk giver. She who brings back the Sun.
Offer us your magical flight that we may celebrate the joy of new beginnings.
That we may know the light will return.
We call to Reindeer-Mother.
Hail and welcome.

Body of Ceremony

Light the Reindeer-Mother candle. Ceremony consists of *gift giving*.

Invite each guest to offer an energetic gift; words, poems, stories, offering of hopes or even a dance. For, as the Mother gives us life and nurtures us always, we must be able to nurture each other.

Bonus Ceremony Meditation Connection

Bring your awareness back to your breath. Close your eyes and connect once more with winter.
Feel and see yourself sitting or standing in the forest.
The trees are bare, all but the evergreens who stand tall, flocked with fresh fallen snow.
The ground is covered with a thick blanket of white.
As you inhale and exhale, you can see your breath.
The forest is calm and very quiet.
Peaceful.
You stand and breathe it all in.
Then you begin to hear footsteps moving through the snow, with a crunch, crunch, crunch.
You see shadows moving through the trees.
Shadows of reindeer.

They move slowly and with caution. Approaching you who stands still in the center of them all.
They have formed a great circle around you.
You should feel uneasy but you do not. You feel safe and held.
Looking before you, the herd parts and a figure approaches.
A reindeer standing on her hind legs, walking as if human. Maybe her legs are human?
She approaches.
The Reindeer-Mother.
Spend a few moments connecting with her calm, serene and loving energy
(pause – before coming back to the space, awake, eyes open).

Fill each Other's Cups and Light the Yule Log

While there are many ways to prep a Yule log, depending on one's tradition, the key is to remember that this is your ceremony, so always trust your instincts and set your intention.

In our wolf pack we have a ceremonial Yule log that has spots carved for candles that we light during our annual ceremony. In my intimate family, we actually burn a Yule log in our wood burning stove. So know that there really is no set way. At least not one that you will be graded upon.

Do it your way! Once the Yule log is lit, offer a toast of good cheer. After all, Yule is a time of celebrating the Sun's return and what does the Sun bring with it? Warmth, light and joy.

When doing a ceremonial toasting, make sure that everyone has a cup or chalice. Take turns filling up each other's chalice or cup and then take turns offering a toast out loud to everyone in attendance. This can take some time if there are quite a few guests, so my suggestion is to take sips after each toast!

Sing a Song of Merriment

Yule is a time of caroling! Nothing unites a group of people more and keeps them all in ceremony mind than raising voices together in song.

Sing a holiday song! There are numerous seasonal songs that have been adapted for Pagan sabbats.

The key is to spend time together as a community/pack/coven/grove in celebration and to bring warmth to each other.

Activating the Bards

While everyone is gathered in ceremony, this is a great time to share stories, similar to how the bards would travel and share offerings of song or stories.

Maybe you have a myth or legend about the Reindeer-Mother that you would like to share?

Offer Gratitude and Open the Container

Now that you have spent time honoring Reindeer-Mother by sharing joy and warmth with your community/pack/coven/grove, you are ready to bid farewell.

Offer Reindeer-Mother gratitude and release her in your own way and in honor of your own tradition.

Do the same with the directional elements and animal archetypes for each.

> "Our lives move in the direction
> of our strongest thoughts."
> **Craig Groeschel**

IMBOLC AND GREAT MOTHER BEAR CEREMONY

Take some time to prepare your ritual space. Do you have a table that you can use as an altar or focal point for your magick? The intent with this ritual is to awaken the Great Mother Bear within to bring a calm, gentle reassurance that you possess within you the strength and might of bear.

It is time to leave the dark of her cave and look forward to the spark within, that quickening of the intentions you will plant this year.

Please remember that it is not of vital importance that you create an altar. For you are the altar. All the tools you need to connect and activate magick within you and around you is already at your fingertips.

As a ritual priestess, I find that the creating process of ritual work IS the ritual. For me, tangible things such as altars create a space for ceremony that I can feel, see and touch. Activating the senses allows me to really experience the magick I am creating.

Please honor your own path and trust your instinctual gut – for you are animal and you already know in your gut what to do.

It may help to read through the meditation and options given before gathering your supplies for this ritual.

Altar Set Up

Green, white, gold or yellow cloth, directional items that represent the elements air, fire, water, earth and spirit, candles of white and red, any fresh seasonal flowers or greenery, pictures or bear figurines.

Create the Container

Typically, Wiccans and most Pagans do their ritual work in a sanctioned space or cast circle to house their magick and allow them a container to do their ceremony in.

While not necessary, as you are the creatrix of your ritual and your intuition will be your guide, please honor your space and your tradition. The key is to really create a time to allow yourself to connect with the Great Bear Mother undisturbed.

Smudge and Bless

As an herbalist, part of my ritual birthing process is to create a loose incense blend that honors my intention. It is the smoke from these incenses that will be utilized to clear the air and help set the tone of the ceremony.

For the Great Mother Bear, I will use some or all of the following herbs: juniper berries, astragulus root, sandalwood, lavender, rose petals, rose hips, yarrow and ginger root.

Communicate your Needs

Part of being a creatrix is expressing one's individual needs. If you have others in your home, please communicate to them that you will need to be undisturbed.

Turn off your electronics and then set your intention. Write down on a piece of paper or carve into an intentional candle your specific intent to call upon bear as Great Mother.

Begin within the Cave

Make sure the room you are in is quite dark.

With your eyes closed, sitting in front of your altar (if you have created one), bring your focus to your breath. Take a nice slow and controlled inhale to the count of five…

Pause for five counts and then exhale out to the count of five.… Hold for five counts and then repeat. By focusing on your breath, you enter the realm and magic of being active in the present moment. Allow your physical body to relax all tension with each exhale.

Repeat this breath pattern for five sequences.

Begin to breathe at your own pace, slow and relaxed with each inhale and exhale.

Here in the dark, picture in your mind's eye that you are lying in a cave. Feel the dirt beneath you as you are lying here. It is completely quiet in the cave with the only sound coming from you as you inhale and exhale. Alone in this cave, in the dark, you are in a space of calm.

Nothing exists but this cave, you and this moment.

(pause)

There may be an unnerving sensation you come upon you as sit here in this dark cave.

But all life begins in the dark of the great cave of our mother's womb, so here you sit, knowing you are once again safe and held within the Great Mother, she as you define her to be.

In your mind's eye, allow yourself to take inventory of your winter. Has it been long, cold and lonely? Has it been restful? Have you been able to really spend time on your inner-ness as a means of devotion to yourself as a creatrix and powerhouse? Or have you exhausted yourself with worry, stresses and the demands each day places upon you?

(pause)

Are you ready for the shift in seasons?

Are you ready to plant new seeds, new intentions and help them grow to fruition?

Sitting here in the dark of the cave, alone with your thoughts, shift from focusing on the winter to moving towards the new possibilities of spring. What is coming your way? Are you excited?

(pause)

Within you there is a quickening, a stirring. You feel a strong urge to stand up and leave the cave.

As if something is pulling you – inviting you to the outdoors.

In your mind's eye, you stand up. Completely naked in this cave, you make your way towards the opening. You seek the light of day that is getting brighter and brighter with each step that you take, until you are standing outside. It is morning and though there are hints of snow on the ground and a slight crisp chill of winter remaining on the wind you welcome the sunlight, you draw down the Sun and, even though naked, you are quite warm.

The forest before you is alive with a chatter of songbirds, tiny green shoots have burst through the once frozen ground and are nodding gently in the breeze. The evergreen trees stand tall and unwavering.

The dirt beneath your feet is spongy and somewhat damp from the melted snow. There is an awakening that has kissed this forest and you can feel the hope and excitement in the air. Winter is over!!!

Before you in the evergreens a large shadow moves, a brown bear is walking towards you.

She moves with slow, steady and precise steps. Her large padded paws sinking into the damp, spongy ground with each step she takes. She is no threat to you and you welcome her as an old friend as kin. She is the Great Mother Bear who welcomes you each year at the beginning of spring.

She greets you with tenderness and as she stands on her hind legs, she is only slightly taller than you. She welcomes you with her large arms and you embrace her.

Feeling the warmth of her fur as she holds you. She nuzzles your neck with her large nose and mouth. Kisses from the Mother as only a mother gives.

After her embrace, she moves to sit before you and you join her on the forest floor. She asks you how your winter rest was and listens intently like a mother to your woes, your trials and your joys.

She asks you if you are ready for this new season and all that it has to offer you, if you are willing to share your intentions with her? You speak to her freely with joy, for you really do have many new seeds to plant this year and you are ready to set those into motion.

After hearing you, she offers a smile and your own set of paws. One thick padded paw for each hand and foot, complete with sharp curved claws. With these she says you can dig in and get to work.

Next she offers you your own bear hide, thick, heavy and as you stand to put it on you, find that it fits perfectly. "With this I offer you strength and protection for there may be times as you move forward that you feel alone, but you will never be alone, for I am always watching over you from up above."

Next she offers you a necklace made from your bear ancestors' teeth. As she places it around your neck, she reminds you that there will be times you may need to show some teeth and defend your rights fiercely but you will know when and you will be prepared. Armed with the essence of bear from the Great Mother Bear, you are more confident than ever to leave winter behind and move towards all the many possibilities that this new season has to offer.

Bring your awareness back to your breath. Consciously focus on your inhale and exhale.

Allow Bear Mother to remain with you or to return back to the cosmos knowing you can call upon her at any time when you have need. With your focus on your breath, you move back to the present, feeling your fingers, your toes and your physical body in perfect order. You awaken.

***

- Light your candles and, as you do, offer gratitude to Bear Mother for her many gifts and her reassurance. How will you honor these gifts?

- Take some time here at your altar, in your ritual space and journal your encounter with the Great Mother Bear. Be as detailed as you can.
- Sit in your ritual space and speak aloud your intentions. What seeds will you be planting this year? You may even decide to light a candle for each intention spoken.
- Optional: gather seeds and small pots, don't forget the dirt. As you place each seed in its pot, speak out loud the intentions you are setting this year, then tuck the seed in and allow water to activate each seed. Call to Bear Mother to bless your seeds as intentions you are setting this year:

> "Great Mother Bear – she of great strength and stature
> gentle one who watches from stars above
> Bless these seeds and see them as my intentions.
> Help me to dig in with sharp claws and do the work of follow through.
> Bless my season as it begins with confidence, renewal and hope.
> Great Mother Bear. Help me to grow. Help me to thrive. Help me to blossom.
> For I am your cub."

COMPLETE YOUR CEREMONY

Ritual/ceremonies need some kind of completion. Once you have connected to Bear Mother and planted either your energetic seeds of intention or your physical seeds, it is always good to give an offering back to the Earth Mother and Bear Mother.

A pouring of libation, sprinkle of incense and a sending of energy down into the land itself where it can spread to the community, are all excellent ways of completing your magick.

When honoring the Great Bear Mother, you are embracing within the mirror she is holding of one that nurtures, loves, supports and encourages as mother archetype. She is the divine feminine. We all come from a mother, who came from a mother, who came from a mother....

Was the very (first ever) mother a great bear that came down from the cosmos? Many of our ancestors believed that we did in fact descend from the Great Bear Mother. Why is this so farfetched? Is it mythical or just a pretty legend?

When a female bear shows up as a mirror, it can very well be an opportunity to heal the mother wound as you define that. Maybe it's time to start nurturing yourself? There are many reasons why a female bear would come to you in the meadow of connection. But ultimately, you are the one that will have to sit with that mirror and really look into it. How are you being given an opportunity to work with such a strong, powerful yet gentle predator seen as a Mother?

If you are in a relationship with someone who has made connection with a female bear as their mirror, how can you honor that? How can you help them to secure this relationship and nurture themselves?

In relationships, we are taught that they are 50/50, which is a very outdated way of viewing things. In essence, that mentality is asking us to simply give just half of ourself and our partner only give half. Relationships on an intimate level are not to be half assed. So I adopt the 100/100 belief in my relationship. Give your full self, all of it! Then allow your partner a space to do the same. Limit the expectations, obligations and stipulations and simply allow for a space where you can both show up as your full fucked up glorious authentic selves.

So if your partner makes connection with a very large female bear, it would be a good idea to give them some space. Each bear person deserves a cave where they can hibernate, go within and percolate ways to nurture and provide some self-care. Each bear person also deserves patience as bear people tend to outwardly appear as if they are moving slowly, it is important to remember that each step they take is determined and precise. Be sure to limit the desire to make comparisons or judgments.

Again, as a wolf person, I have a tendency to nip at my bear man especially when I am in a mood to get things done. So patience is vital! Also I limit my show of teeth and my bark when, as a bear, he needs to walk away to figure things out. Patience and one's own cave really honors the bear in your relationships.

> "It's better to be absolutely ridiculous
> than to be absolutely boring."
>
> *Marilyn Monroe*

OSTARA AND THE MAD MARCH HARE CEREMONY

As I begin to journey with you down the rabbit hole into hare medicine and magick, it is the beginning of March. The winds of change are blowing with a vengeance as if to demand winter to exit and make room for spring.

March is an eventful month! The earth seems to wake up and become alive again after her rest in the cold winter months. With this increase of longer days and the snow beginning to dwindle, a deep excitement begins to build. Most people begin plotting or even planting their gardens and there is an ever abundant desire to go outside.

Spring has always been one of my favorite seasons. Here in the High Desert of southern Utah where I make my home, the actual spring season doesn't last very long as our winter can often drag out into mid April or early May, then in two weeks the weather is hot and summer prevails. The magic of spring is often intoxicating.

As a priestess devoted to Paganism, I love helping the Wheel of the Year turn by decorating my home, yard and goddess temple with all things spring. Pastel flowers, new plants and herbs in the garden and, of course, plenty of hares!

THE WHEEL OF THE YEAR

Crafting a Ceremony to Embrace the Energy of Hare (this ritual can be done with family or community):

- Decorate your ritual space with all things spring. Be as creative as you wish. In our goddess temple we have directional altars that are all decorated with pastel altar cloths, lots of eggs, flowers and, of course, bunnies.
- Typically Ostara is celebrated right around the spring equinox, close to or on March 21st.

Optional Tools to Enhance the Ritual Experience
1. staff or walking stick (can be decorated in spring flare)
2. reusable black or red eggs (preferably wood ones that have been pre-painted black)
3. white, gold or silver markers
4. loose comfortable clothing
5. stuffed toy hare
6. votive candle to represent the mad hare

- This is a very lively ritual and can be done in the center of your property. With your staff in hand, move through the *Breathing into Hare Mind* meditation to help you and your community or family anchor into the intention of calling to the hare and waking up the Mother (Gaia, Earth, Nature) in celebration of spring.
- Depending on your practice, you create your container facing the direction you honor first. For some it is the north, others the north-east and for some the east. The key is to honor and create your sacred container in your own way as it is your magick you are working. Now for the fun part!!!
- Standing facing the directions, you tap your staff upon the earth three times, as if you are knocking on the door to the underworld and the one leading the rituals calls out:

> "Wake up Mother Earth, the time has come! Spring has sprung and there is much to be done!"

- Repeat this call to each direction in your own way and own style. At the end of each calling, cheer, holler, jump up and down, make a mad ruckus as if the noise will stir the sleeping mother of spring to awaken.

- Once the directions have been awakened, you are ready to call upon the mad hare of spring, or if you prefer; the Goddess Ostara. This is best done intuitively. Be sure to light the candle to ignite the essence of their energy.
- Now that your container and circle have been cast, sit upon the earth and share the story of the Eostre hare. Be enthusiastic and have fun! Springtime is all about play, new beginnings and excitement.
- Make sure that everyone is given a black or red egg. These are intention eggs and will be taken home and placed upon one's altar or kept in a sacred space or even buried in the center of your yard.
- Think of the seeds of intention that you set back in early February with Mother Bear (Chapter Two) and now with your marker, write down or create a sigil that brings those seedling intentions to life. For example, if you set the intention of taking better care of your health on your egg, you may write down how you are taking care of your health. Be creative! With spring being the time of fertility and abundance, think back on how you have blossomed since Imbolc. Decorate your egg.

(The colors red and black both symbolize internal work. Red for the blood within us that flows and black to honor the dark of the underworld where all things grow. Remember a seed will only germinate in the dark)

Optional Ritual Ideas
- Recite the story of the Eostre hare.
- Egg hunts with gemstones in each egg, or an inspirational word.
- Egg dying with natural roots and herbs.
- Games of croquet.
- Tea parties.

THE LEGEND OF THE EOSTRE HARE
(A RETELLING BY LADY WOLF)

Long, long ago, the land was filled with magic and the gods and goddesses of old walked amongst us. One such goddess was

THE WHEEL OF THE YEAR

Eostre, she who was said to be most beautiful of all, her hair long and flowing with tiny flowers woven within. She was most kind and most loving. Everywhere she stepped, flowers would grow, plants would thrive and all the animals would flock to her.

Eostre had one job and that was to wake up and greet all the plants and animals each year on the first day of spring. One particular year, she found herself out in the middle of a beautiful forest. As she walked from plant to plant and animal to animal saying "wake up little one, spring is here," she came upon a tiny wounded bird. Eostre loved all animals and plant life and she felt so sorry for the little bird with its broken wing that she knew she had to help it; otherwise it would surely become prey to a nearby predator.

So, the Goddess Eostre picked up the small bird and turned it into a hare because hares are quick and can escape danger. The hare jumped from her arms and ran off into the forest and Eostre went about her job again of waking all things up for spring.

The hare though was so moved and filled with gratitude, that the goddess had taken time out of her most busy day to show him such compassion, that he wanted to take her a gift to show his appreciation. Because he was once a bird, he had retained his ability to lay eggs. So, he laid her an egg and began to paint it in the colors and shades of spring. He then hopped to where the Goddess Eostre was resting at the end of her most busy day and he placed the egg at her feet.

Eostre was so moved by this gesture that she asked the hare if each year on this day – the first of spring – he would gift painted eggs to all the children that they may embrace and feel the magic of spring. This is how the Eostre hare was employed by the Goddess of Spring Eostre and why today we have the Easter Bunny.

- One of the most commonly asked questions I get after telling this story is "how come the Easter Bunny is a boy when as a bird it was a female?" The answer is really quite simple; the hare, in myths and legends throughout almost all pantheons, is androgynous which by definition is "something that has both female and male traits." So yes, the Eostre hare is a male that has retained its female trait of laying eggs as a bird.

- Complete your ritual by offering thanks and gratitude to the mad hare for his whimsy, abundant joy and unpredictable wildness.
- Offer thanks and gratitude to the directions in your own way.
- Celebrate with libations and festive foods. Nothing grounds one better after ritual than tasty food shared with good people. Think deviled eggs, egg salad, potato salad, fresh greens and plenty of Easter sweets.

BELTANE WITH BUTTERFLIES

Intention
For this ceremony, the intent and focus is on activating the Fae through whimsy, dancing the maypole and making merry.

This ceremony will be outside.

Maypole Prepping
First things first; find a pole! Preferably one that is over six feet tall. Remember that in order for the maypole to stand erect (yes, pun intended) you will need to dig a hole about twelve inches deep.

Do not yet place the pole into the hole – that will happen during the ceremony. Have at least two large buckets filled with dirt ready to go when it's time to tuck the pole in. Gather ribbons of every color.

Hole Prepping
Once you have dug the hole, create a circle around it with rocks or freshly picked flowers.

This hole will become the focal point for the ceremony.

Working Altar Set Up
Set up your outdoor altar somewhere near the ceremony hole. You will want it to be in a location that is assessable for guests. Cover your altar with bright colored cloth and a vase of fresh flowers. You will need a bowl or chalice to hold water and loose incense for smudging and clearing.

You will also need about six bowls (I use crystal bowls) that you will fill with herbs that will be used to bless the ceremonial hole. Stones can be used as well, along with messages of intentions.

Suggested herbs: mint-abundance, rosemary-remembrance, rose petals-love, calendula-strength, yarrow-protection, catnip-play.

Ceremonial Attire
Guests should be encouraged to wear flowing, colorful, whimsical outfits.
- Optional: buy bulk fairy wings from a dollar store and gift them to each guest as they begin to line up. Or invite guests to buy and wear their own fairy wings.

Ceremonial Procession
Have them line up and enter the ceremonial circle by walking around and around the ceremonial hole in the center. If you have musically inclined guests, have them drum, rattle and sing as they group in circles.

This very act creates a stirring of energy that will spiral around and around. As guests are walking, have someone stand in the center holding the bowl or chalice of water and, using a freshly picked flower, begin to dip the flower into the water and sprinkle the water around and as each guest walks by. Have another guest stand near the working altar and, with the loose incense, smudge as the guests circle.

COLLECTION OF SABBAT CEREMONIES

Create the Container
In your own way and honoring your own tradition, call to the directional elements.

Welcome the animals of each direction with song or summoning, in accordance with your tradition.

Welcome Summoning to Butterflies
With everyone standing in a circle forming an outer ring around the ceremonial hole, pour the sacred water from chalice into the hole as a blessing. Invite guests to hold hands and create a soft low hum.

Feel as the hum rises and moves around the circle. Once you feel the energy peak – whoever is calling moves to stand in the center – with arms outstretched, reaching up.

> "We stand as a circle within a circle to assist with the great turning of the wheel. We call to the butterflies. Those who fly from flower to flower and mirror to us the magick of transformation.
> We welcome your play and ask that you inspire us to be more jovial and find joy in the little things.
> We welcome you to fly amongst us. May we too have wings to enjoy the merriment of the season.
> Hail and welcome the butterflies."

BODY OF CEREMONY

Invite guests to activate their inner butterflies and select a handful or bowl of herbs from the working altar. This should be playful and fun as guests circle and scatter the herbs around the inner circle and in the ceremonial hole.

As they sprinkle, have them express out loud and share the things that bring them joy and pleasure in life (if you have a large enough group you may want to split them in half – with one half scattering the herbs and the other half placing the pole).

The Dance
With the herbs scattered and the hole blessed with song or chant, the time has come to tie on the ribbons. Split your group into two – one half holds the pole at an angle while the other half starts tying ribbons on the end that will be in the sky.

Once the ribbons are tied on, gently place the pole within the hole, use the two buckets filled with dirt to tuck in the pole. Holding onto the ribbons, you will alternate your dance. Every other person turns to the left, while the other turns to the right. Move over and under, around and around.

While you dance the dance, you can sing, chant or have music playing. Make merry! Laugh, be eccentric and feel as if you have the wings of a butterfly and just fly over and under, around and around. Once the end of the ribbons is reached and your dance is complete, spend time as a community admiring your maypole.

Optional: You may want to do a meditation activation and call upon butterfly to gift you wings that you may see the abundance in your life and celebrate joy (meditation can be found in Chapter Ten).

Open the Container
Offer gratitude to butterfly, the directions and elemental animals.

Feast and Make Merry
It is tradition at Beltane to have a bonfire and a big feast with plenty of dancing.

Working Beltane Altar

Bonus Community or Family Celebrations

- Beltane is an excellent time to make homemade prayer flags and decorate your yard and entrance with them. Use bright colored fabric and invite everyone to paint an image that brings them joy or paint sigils that invoke abundance!

  Be creative and add some colorful flare to your event.

- Another fun activity is a community planting day. Create a new planter each Beltane and invite guests to bring perennial seeds or plants and watch over the years as Beltane magick returns to bless the land.

  Some of my favorite perennial plants are mugwort, columbines, morning glories (they do take over though) comfrey, mint and goblin flowers.

  To make this event even more playful, invite guests to wear fairy wings as they plant.

- Beltane punch: with the heat of the Sun inviting passion into the lives of all the animals and humans making a festive beverage can add to the occasion. I love a good sangria!

> One bottle of red wine.
> One small bottle of brandy or rum.
> Freshly picked berries (strawberries, raspberries, blackberries, blueberries).
> Soak the berries in the brandy or rum overnight.
> Next morning combine all ingredients and add some Fresca or lemonade.
> I like to put edible freshly picked flowers on the top of the punch to add some garden pizzazz.

- Make flower crowns! Everyone needs to feel like royalty! Gather everyone together and use either fresh flowers or fake; sit in a circle and craft a decorative crown.

  These would be perfect to wear during the ceremony!

LITHA WITH HUMMINGBIRDS

Hummingbird

For this summertime ceremony, hummingbird represents the quick and fleeting heat of the season. Hummingbirds are resilient, agile and waste no time.

We will call to hummingbird as teacher, mentor, messenger and guide and ask it to mirror to all participating that there is time to visit the beauty of every flower, make the most of each summer day – we just have to get up a bit earlier and greet the Sun.

Altar Set Up

A bright cloth that represents the colors and heat of the Sun. Lots of fresh picked flowers. Statue(s) or images of the Sun, faeries and hummingbirds. Gold, red, orange stone people; candles and copper or brass chalice, cauldron or bowl. Fill the bowl with different kinds of berries.

Intention for Ceremony

Litha, or summer solstice, is a time of great abundance. The Sun stands in its highest position, watching over and ensuring the growth of all below. The days are longer and the energy is very powerful, exciting, joyful and bright. It's a time to celebrate the fertility that has been birthed since Beltane.

Great Mother Earth is showing us just how colorful and alive she is and we can be too if we get outside, work hard and devote ourselves to living in harmony with Nature – we can truly step into a more conscious connection and not only see the magick of Litha, but emulate it both within ourselves and around.

Daytime Ceremony

While most high holy seasonal sabbat ceremonies occur in the evening (most likely to accommodate everyone's work schedule); Litha is a perfect sabbat to celebrate in the peak of the heat of the day. Or right at sunrise.

This ceremony is centered on greeting the Sun but only you know the weather and climate of where you live, so keep your magick anchored into the ground you actually walk upon when crafting and creating your ceremony.

Smudge and Water Bless

Be creative with your smudge and always use locally grown herbs from your garden if you can.

At Litha, I have an abundance of plants in full bloom in the garden. It is their essence I want to activate and honor, so I craft a loose incense the day before ceremony, gathering much yarrow, mint, mugwort and other plants (that are safe for burning as sacred smudge) and I then run them through a dehydrator.

I always keep a large amount set aside so that I can create a tea that will be used during ceremony for the water blessing and ceremonial libations. Whatever you decide to use, you are setting the intention to enter into a ceremony or ritual mindset free from ego, negativity and the chaos of life. So, smudge and water bless in your own way.

Ground and Anchor Meditation

Once all guests have arrived (hopefully dressed in their most colorful summertime wares) and have been smudged and water blessed, invite them to gather in circle.

Again this sabbat is best outside. Welcome the guests and begin.

"Here we stand, heart to heart, and hand in hand. Let us breathe our intention into this land, the sky and the center of our circle. Taking a nice slow inhale, and nice slow exhale, allow your eyes to close as we enter a state of presence. Simply bringing our focus to our breath. Allow yourself to connect with the ground beneath and the sky above you. As you breathe deep, feel the Sun as it kisses your skin with its heat. Feel the Earth as she pulls your energy downward creating an anchor. Allow your mind to clear as you simply breathe in and breathe out."

Create the Container
In your own way and honoring your own tradition, create the container for your magick ceremony by calling to the directions and welcoming the elements and guardians associated with each.

Call to Hummingbird
To enhance the energy and create a more dramatic shift, invite each guest to begin a soft low hum.

This act of humming keeps people in the present moment and mimics the hum of the hummingbird. As guests hum, the one leading ceremony calls out loud to the hummingbird.

"We call to hummingbird, bringer of joy and good luck. With open hearts and merriment we sing the hum of the hummingbird and welcome the energy of abundance into our lives on this day as we celebrate Litha/summer solstice.

We call to hummingbird and as that you visit with each of us as you do each flower in the garden. Remind us of how short summer is and encourage us to embrace your passion, agility and determination to experience as much as we can, laugh often and live passionately this time of year so that no moment is wasted.

We honor you, we hum for you and we welcome you Great Hummingbird."

Body of Ceremony
Litha is a great time for a dance party around a bonfire a time to sing and make merry and share each other's stories of abundance, hopes and dreams.

Welcome everyone to sit upon the earth, remaining in circle and offer up a time of open share. Invite guests one at a time to share something that they have accomplished so far this year that started as a tiny seed and is now starting to bloom.

With each offering, pass one of the bowls filled with berries around the circle so that everyone can enjoy the abundance and sweetness that comes from allowing each other a space to share, be heard and be celebrated. This also creates a 'buzz' or 'hum' of an energetic vibe within the circle.

Another option is to cheer, hoot, holler, yip and yowl in celebration following each guest's share of abundance.

Option #2

This option comes from the midsummer event I attended at Zsuzsanna Budapest's home earlier this year. Gather guests in a circle and, in the center, have a large cauldron with charcoal disks lit.

After each guest has shared their stories of growth they have experienced so far in the year, they add a small pinch of frankincense to the cauldron.

When one burns frankincense (which is a resin from the Bosweilla tree which has been burned for centuries and is known to shift the brainwaves into a more calm and open state) the psychoactive shift in brainwaves allows one to absorb and focus deeper.

When you burn frankincense in a ceremony; that very act becomes the ceremony.

Meditation to Activate Connection with Hummingbird

After everyone has had an opportunity to share, invite everyone to get comfortable, close their eyes and shift their focus back to their breath one more time.

Breathing nice and slow with intention to calm their mind and enter a meditative state.

Here in this state of mind, the body is completely relaxed.

The mind becomes centered and open to receive messages and insights.

Here in this state, in your mind's eye, where all things are possible, see yourself sitting in the center of a flower garden. The garden is filled with flowers of every variety. The petals are bright, vibrant and the smell is intoxicating.

This garden represents your life; ever abundant and full of vigor.

This garden is alive, healthy and in full bloom. There are bees buzzing and with each breath of wind the smell of the flowers awakens your inner mind to a realization that there is much to celebrate.

You hear a loud humming and you see that a hummingbird is in the flower garden.

Then another hummingbird appears. More and more join you in the garden.

With the flower garden in full bloom and the buzzing and humming of bees and hummingbirds, you feel as if you too are vibrating. Maybe you feel like joining in. Offering a buzz or a hum.

One hummingbird comes right up to your face and slows its brisk hovering to make direct eye contact with you, as if it is telling you that even though summer is quick and fleeting with much to do, there is time to pause and enjoy the moments. There is time to stop and visit each flower.

Spend a few moments here with hummingbird. Connect.

(pause)

As the wind shifts direction, the hummingbird flies away and leaves you once more to sit in the center of your garden. As you gaze around and take notice of all the beautiful flowers, you smile.

Life is truly abundant! You sit in gratitude and reflection as you take inventory of all the seeds that you planted at Imbolc and all those seeds that have come into full bloom. Your smile radiates even more when you realize that soon the harvest season will be upon us and each of these flowers will drop seeds onto the ground that will sprout and bloom in the following year.

You are filled with peace knowing that the Wheel of the Year continues to turn both around you and within you – for you are one with Nature and all things are connected.

Pause for Reflection

Following meditation, you may want to invite guests to share their experience with hummingbird and their garden. Or you may want to invite them to sit and journal.

Open the Container

Invite guests to stand and offer gratitude to hummingbird, the directions and elements associated with each in their own way and honoring their own tradition.

Feast and Make Merry

It is always fun to celebrate with food and a bonfire!

   Invite guests to bring a potluck seasonal dish to share following the ceremony. Berries, pies and colorful salads are all delightful at this time of year.

Another fun way to celebrate Litha, following the ceremony, is to invite guests to help make treats for the birds. Such as pine cones smeared with peanut butter and then rolled in bird seeds, which are then hung upon the trees. You can craft a community aviary! Don't forget to prepare a couple feeders for the hummingbirds. Making crafts following ceremony creates unity and helps each individual to anchor into and physically feel the intent and energy of the ceremony.

Great Websites for Guides to Making a Hummingbird Feeder

https://reachinghappy.com/learning/diy-humming-bird-feeder/
https://suncatcherstudio.com/birds/homemade-hummingbird-feeders/

LUGHNASADH AND EAGLE

Eagle

For this ceremony, eagle represents strength, confidence and seeing one's abundant soul harvest through a 'bird's eye view.'

When we call to eagle, we do so from a state of honor and remembrance, for eagles have been deemed *messengers of the gods* since the beginning.

Altar Set Up

Gold, red, orange or yellow altar cloth; candle; image or figure of eagle; harvest vegetables (fresh is best); flowers (freshly picked).

The altar should look like a cornucopia of freshly gathered herbs, fruits and veggies. I enjoy making mandalas with freshly picked herbs and placing a plate in the center for the candle.

For this ceremony, utilizing feathers is a great way to set the tone for the intention. Once you have taken time to create your altar and set your intention of celebrating the FIRST of the three harvest sabbats, you are ready to begin.

Intention for Ceremony

The intention is to assist in the turning of the great wheel by focusing attention on what you as an individual or collectively as a coven/grove/pack or community have harvested so far.

Lughnasadh is a time of reflection on one's soul harvest.

Smudge and Water Bless

With Lughnasadh being a harvest celebration, making a loose incense blend from all the herbs you have growing and available is a great way to connect and honor the land and the season you are celebrating. Also, collecting water from a natural source is best!

For our Lughnasadh celebration, we made a lovely blend of mugwort, catnip, mint, yarrow, comfrey and dandelion for our incense and our water blessing was actually fresh rainwater, as it was raining when we began our ceremony.

Ground and Anchor Meditation

Inviting guests to participate fully in ceremony is the best way to offer them an experience into the realm of the liminal. After your container has been cast, invite guests to close their eyes and focus on their breath.

This act of disconnecting from ego mind and moving within is simple when we close our eyes. When we intentionally feel the wind within our body – our breath move in and out – we disconnect from wandering thoughts and we enter pure magick and that is being fully present.

Oftentimes, the best grounding and anchoring meditation is just that; simply closing one's eyes and focusing on one's inhale and exhale for about five minutes. If you would like to connect deeper, then create a guided meditation that fits the flow and intention of the ceremony. Be open to intuition.

Create the Container

In your own way and tradition, create your container for your magick. In my community, which we fondly call the 'wolf pack', we cast our circle with song as our tradition 'desert sage witchcraft' is a very eclectic, Bardic style of magick, anchored into animism.

When we turn to face each direction, we sing a welcome song and call to a local animal that represents and compliments that direction. For example, east-raven, south-lizard, west-toad, north-antelope.

This is something that can be done regardless of where one lives. As witches, you are all familiar with your elemental animal messengers, and if not; this practice gives you an opportunity to connect with your local animal guides.

Call to Eagle

Instead of calling to a god or goddess (such as Lugh the Sun King, or Ceridwen), you will be calling to eagle. With your candle in the center of the ceremony altar, stand with arms outstretched like a great bird about to take flight and, taking a nice slow inhale, on your exhale begin your summoning:

> On this the day of the first harvest we stand with arms outstretched like a winged bird to call upon
> Great Eagle. We call to you who represents strength, wisdom, confidence and nobility.
> Great Eagle who is brave, bold, victorious and free.

We welcome your talons that remind us to dig in deep into the earth, for the harvest is upon us.

We welcome your wings that give us flight to rise above and see with new perspective all that we have sown, all that we will gather. For our soul's harvest is abundant!

We welcome your sharp beak that mirrors our wit, our passion and our capability to tear into all that we wish to savor in this, the time of harvest.

Hail and welcome Great Eagle who soars on high.

Light the Candle of the Eagle

Body of Ceremony

Invite guests to settle in and take a few moments to reflect upon all that they have harvested since Imbolc. What seeds were planted with Great Mother Bear that have come to fruition?

Invite guest to share, one by one, their soul's harvest. Reminding them that this is only the beginning of the harvest season and that there is much more to come.

Optional Ideas

Invite guests to take time to write down on a piece of paper their soul's harvest.

Eagle Shapeshifting Meditation

Now that guests have reflected upon their soul's harvest, offer them time to connect with eagle through meditation, visualization and shapeshifting.

This allows each person a more intimate experience and hopefully additional insight into what they have really harvested so far.

While not necessary; having background music or white noise really does help when leading a group meditation. My favorite ceremony music is from the band 'Wardruna'.

> "With eyes closed, we begin our journey towards connecting with eagle as both mirror and guide. We bring our focus to our breath. Inhaling to the count of four and exhaling to the count of four (repeat at least five times). Allow your body to create its own wave of rhythmic breaths as you intentionally exhale any tension or strain from your physical body. With each inhale, you offer permission to release as you exhale out and away anything that no longer serves your highest good. With your physical

body relaxed, you are ready to move deeper into your subconscious. As you send your breath down to your feet, feel as they shift into thick, sharp talons of an eagle. Feel as eagle energy moves through your body and your legs shorten, your flesh begins to soften as it allows feathers to push through; covering you from ankle to brow. Feel your arms stretching outward, and as they do, your fingers pull inwards and feathers reach out. Your bones shift and your wings extend. Allow this sensation to move down your back, all the way down to your tail bone – where tail feathers push out.

You breathe in deeply through the nostrils of eagle, as your nose and mouth embrace the elongated shape of a beak; hard and sharp. Your eyes narrow outward seeing things from all angles, new angles. … You may feel your head moving meticulously from side to side, up and down – tight, clicking movements that allow you to observe on a new level.

Here you are perched as eagle. Feel your great talons clamp down, grasping a thick branch at the top of a great tree. You gaze down and you see your life. Your harvest lies before you; tiny but abundant, for you see it with a bird's eye view; looking down, all around. With your wings outstretched, you soar upon the winds and gently, as if floating, you get a closer look. As you fly downwards, you see all that you have planted, all that you have watered – all those seeds that you have energetically, spiritually and physically invested time and energy into. They have grown!

They are ready to enjoy, to harvest, to sow. You see so much more with a bird's eye view.

With the confidence of eagle, you fly over your garden of life and give yourself permission to really see all that you have grown and all that you are ready to now harvest. With the eyes of eagle, you see with those 'all seeing eyes' that you have much to celebrate and much more to harvest and gain in the months to come.

(pause)

Now that you have seen your harvest, you land upon the ground in your garden of life.

Feel as your talons sink into the rich dirt. Sending breath down, you feel as the talons become one with the earth and your own feet push through. Feel your toes, your feet, standing upon the dirt. Feel as you flesh your way back into your body and the feathers fade – your legs becoming human once more. You breathe with intention into your wings and feel as your bones shift and the feathers fall as your skin pushes them out and away. Your fingers flexing and bending as you begin to take your human shape.

You breathe in deeply and your nose pushes through where there once was a beak. Your eyes soften and shift. With each breath, you come back into your body, knowing eagle is always there when you are in need. But now you shift into your full form. Feeling whole, feeling complete and feeling joy as you breathe in the knowing that you have before you an abundant first harvest with much more to follow."

Pause for Reflection
Now invite guests to further their reflection on their soul's harvest. Maybe eagle showed them more than what they originally saw before the shapeshifting? What work has been done since Imbolc and what harvest is each guest celebrating?

Allow time for each guest to share out loud their harvest. When each guest has an opportunity to share, they offer permission for others to celebrate their own unique soul harvests and when we collectively share our joys, we feed each other.

Optional
Have guests light a candle as they share their soul's harvest.

Opening the Container
In your own way and honoring your own tradition, open the container. Firstly by offering gratitude to eagle for being mirror and teacher, then move onto the directional elements.

End your Ceremony with Feasting
As Lughnasadh is the first of the three harvest celebrations, having a feast is the best way to anchor in after high magick. It is also the perfect way to enjoy the season.

When we come together and share the abundance of the season, we honor our ancestors and each other.

> "Walking, I am listening to a deeper way. Suddenly all my ancestors are behind me.
> Be still, they say. Watch and listen.
> You are the result of the love of thousands."
>
> *Linda Hogan* (1947)

MABON WITH SALMON

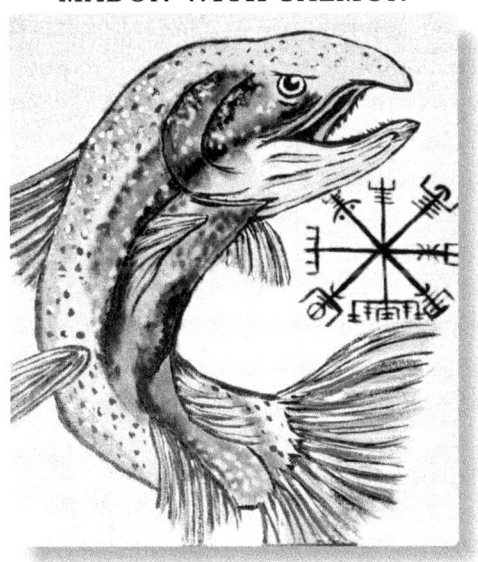

Salmon

The intention with activation connection with salmon is to invite salmon to mirror back to each individual perseverance, determination and hard work.

Salmon is also all about honoring one's ancestry, so this ceremony will begin to help everyone celebrate the legacy of their ancestors and prepare to welcome them home in the upcoming sabbat of Samhain.

Honor the messages from Salmon: Keep going! Don't give up! Follow your own path, do not go with the stream. Be bold, be determined. Go against the stream and challenge yourself. Jump up and out of uncomfortable waters. Activate connection with your ancestors. Take a spiritual journey.

Altar Set Up

> Deep blue altar cloth to represent the water that salmon must swim through.
> A bowl of sea salt or pink Himalayan salt, and a bowl of dried rosemary.
> Markers, small pieces of paper, mod podge, brushes, plenty of tall pillar candles in glass.
> An image of the Vegvisir and/or salmon statue or framed image.
> Plenty of fall colored flowers; fresh, dried or artificial.
> A cornucopia filled with harvest veggies.

Intention for Ceremony

Mabon is often referred to as 'the witches' Thanksgiving.' Creating a ceremony that celebrates the second of the three harvests is a great time to bring friends, family and community together.

Invite guests to bring food to share, preferably food from their garden or prepared fresh by their own hands.

While the intention of this ceremony is to celebrate the second harvest, it is also a time to honor the past, look at one's ancestry and share their journey. Beforehand, do some research. Dig into your past and invite your guests to do the same. Invite them to bring a story of one of their ancestors to share.

How to Prepare for this Ceremony?

This ceremony consists of ancestral work. It would be a good idea to reach out to guests in advance and offer them insight on how to best come prepared.

I love the saying "every journey home, begins at home." When it comes to learning about your own history, it's a good idea to start talking to family members (grandparents, parents, cousins, etc…) who can share their knowledge.

While this may seem like a daunting beginning, if one is unsure of who their biological family is, DNA testing has made this part of the journey easier each year as technology advances. *Ancestry.com* is an incredible site to help one dive in and begin (most ancestry websites are free to use).

Get organized! Once you start swimming in the waters of your ancestry, it helps to have some form of organization – charts or files. The family tree at first can seem to be very basic but once you dive in deeper, you may find this to be just a simple beginning.

The internet has allowed us to gain so much information and knowledge – right at our fingertips. It is a good idea with ancestry to narrow down your searches. For example, are you wanting to discover when and where your family immigrated from? Are you wanting to uncover genetic health traits or are you wanting to make a pilgrimage to where your earliest known ancestors began?

1. Talk to your living family members to begin the process
2. Take a DNA test
3. Organize your information!
4. Narrow down your intentions

Smudge and Water Bless

Take a pinch of the Himalayan salt and/or sea salt and add to your blessing water.

In your own way and honoring your own tradition, smudge and water bless guests as they circle into ceremony space.

Create the Container

In your own way and own tradition, cast your circle. Create your container.

Call to the directions and elemental beings associated with each one.

Call to Salmon

"We call to salmon on this the second harvest sabbat of Mabon.

We welcome the determination, precision and perseverance of Great Salmon and invite salmon to join us as we circle in honor of our ancestors, share their stories and open up the rivers, streams and oceans of connection.

May we take this time of great abundance and see upon whose shoulders we stand.

May we honor the legacy of those who sacrificed much.

May we look to those who pilgrimaged and made sacred journeys focused on preserving one's family.

May we see you as our mirror and may we continue to work hard and be steadfast.

We welcome the Great Salmon of the waters."

Body of Ceremony

Invite guests to select a candle from the altar and be seated.

Holding the candle in their hands, lead them into meditation to awaken salmon mind and activate a journey within.

"With your eyes closed, bring your focus and attention to your breath, taking a nice slow inhale followed by a slow exhale.

Consciously allow each breath to move through your body, creating a rhythm all its own.

In your mind's eye, activate the essence and energy of salmon. You may want to ask yourself, what drives you? What motivates you? What moves you to keep going, even when you are tired?

What currents in the waters of your life are you swimming in? Are you moving upstream?

Or are you simply allowing the current to take you out to sea where you can float?

Take your focus a little bit deeper into your inner waters.

Think of your blood flowing within your veins as your sacred water, the elixir that pumps through you. What lies in the mysteries of your blood? What is it made up of? Who is it made of?

Call to your ancestors, activate your bloodline.

What journey are you going to take to awaken this ancestral connection, and what journey will you take that will allow you to swim home?

Salmon energy is all about honoring one's ancestral medicine and magick.

Holding this candle, circled as family, let us all breathe deep into the depths of our past, our history and begin to understand where we came from.

What struggles did our ancestors meet on their journeys?

How can we learn from them? How can we honor them?"

Open Share

With salmon energy activated and intention candles charged, allow guests time for an open share of stories. Invite guests one at a time to share something about their ancestors.

They can share their DNA lineage, a story told to them by an elder in their family, or even a name of one of their ancestors.

Option

If you do not want to have guests share their ancestry stories, you can share some myths and legends that focus on salmon energy.

As a member of the Bardic Order, sharing stories is a great way of invoking the intention into the ceremony. Be theatrical, sing, make stories, share an offering or sacred libation. One of my favorite stories to share at Mabon is the story of Loki.

When it comes to shapeshifting gods, Loki the Norse trickster is the most often thought of. While admittedly he is not loved and embraced by all, he does possess quite the ability to shift into other shapes to accomplish many tasks, even if most are to avoid the punishments of the other gods.

When diving into Norse mythology, the *Prose Edda* is typically the jumping-off point. This thirteenth century book, written by Icelandic historian, Snorri Sturlluson, is a great source for reading up on the myths and legends of the Norse pantheon. Another favorite of mine is *Norse Mythology* by Neil Gaiman.

The legend goes that Loki, being masterful, cunning and wise, created a brilliant scheme to kill the golden haired and most beloved son of Frigg; Baldur. Knowing that he would be hunted down to his painful death if captured for this heinous act, Loki transformed himself into a salmon. In salmon form, Loki could hide under the water. However, to pass the time, Loki would shift into human form and weave linen twine to create a net so fine that he could catch fish that swam by.

One day while working on his net, he heard the gods approaching and he cast the net into the waters and shifted back into salmon form. The gods discovered this net and knew that Loki must be nearby. They tried repeatedly to catch Loki in the net. Loki, knowing he could be caught in his own net, began to jump high into the air, like the sockeye salmon still do to this day.

As he was leaping up out of the waters, the mighty Thor reached out and grabbed hold of his slippery, scaly prey. Loki was captured. With Thor's mighty grip, he ripped the tail end of the salmon Loki. It is because of Loki that we now have salmon with a split tail and nets for fishing.

Optional Story of the Salmon of Knowledge

In Irish mythology, you read about Fionn Mac Cumhaill and the Salmon of Knowledge. In this legend, it was said amongst the ancient Druids that a salmon lived in the River Boyne in a shallow pool, given shade by a majestic hazel tree. This salmon had eaten nine hazel nuts, giving it the knowledge of the world.

The Druids had prophesied that anyone who could catch and eat this salmon would obtain the world knowledge for themselves. A poet named Finegas, who was well read and said to be all wise, was obsessed with catching the salmon of knowledge. While at the River Boyne, Finegas saw what could only be this infamous salmon swimming in the waters.

The legend also warns that anyone who locks eyes with the salmon would fall into a great slumber. So Finegas made every attempt to catch the fish without making eye contact. He failed and collapsed into a great sleep.

Nearby Fionn, who was the son of a great warrior who had been sent to live with Finegas, saw what happened. He quickly ran to the shore and woke Finegas who, upon awakening, bound his eyes with a cloth and spent hours attempting to catch the salmon.

He did succeed but was so exhausted that he had Fionn cook the fish but warned him to not eat any part of it. Fionn agreed and began to cook the fish. As he was taking it out of the flames, he accidentally burned his finger and blistered immediately.

Not thinking, he quickly reacted by putting his burned thumb into his mouth to cool it off. This simple act of cooling his finger had allowed him to absorb the world knowledge from the salmon.

Crafting the Ancestral Intention Candles

With stories shared and the energy of the ancestors in the space, it's time to craft the candles.

Invite each guest to take one marker and one piece of paper. On each paper, guests will create the Vegvisir – often referred to as the Viking compass, runic compass, Norse protection symbol or Icelandic magical stave.

This sacred symbol (shown above) was carved/inscribed onto shield or skin, typically with blood, as a way of activating a deep knowing that no matter the weather, the waves or the rocks along the journey – the one who wears this symbol or sigil will always find their way home.

The Vegvisir was mentioned in the *Huld* manuscript by Geir Vigusson in 1860 (which was compiled close to eight centuries after the Viking Age ended), in one sentence: "If this sign is carried, one will never lose one's way in storms or bad weather, even when the way is not known."

There really is no concrete evidence that this sigil is of the Viking Age as we really only have this one sentence description. It was also mentioned in the *Galdrakver* by Olgeir Geirsson in 1869, and in another galdrakver (book of spells) by an unknown author. But again, there is no evidence that confirms that this sigil or symbol was ever used by what we refer to as the Vikings.

We can, however, break down the word to help us decipher a more definite meaning. *Vegur* means road and path. *Visir* means path or guide. *Vegur* comes from the Old Norse *Vegr*, meaning to show, point or visit. Basically, according to Wikipedia: "It points someone the right way." In Icelandic, the word means 'guidepost, way finder, signpost.'

Many people have embraced the Vegvisir as their own personal compass in spell work, Icelandic witchcraft practitioners, Neopagans, heathen Asatru practices, and also in body art in the form of tattoos. I personally have the Vegvisir tattooed on my right forearm as a reminder that no matter what journey I embark upon, I will always find my way back home, whether physically or, most often; spiritually. The Vegvisir has been embraced as a spiritual compass or pilgrimage compass.

Once the Vegvisir has been drawn, invite guests to glue the sigil onto their candles. They may want to inscribe the names of their ancestors as well. The key is to be creative and to enjoy the work collectively. Use the mod podge to secure the sigil. Then have each guest place their candle on the altar.

Open the Container
Offer gratitude to salmon in your own way and honoring your own tradition.

Offer gratitude to the directions and elemental beings associated with each.

Witches' Thanksgiving Feast or the Feast of Mabon
Now it's time to enjoy the Feast – to make merry and gather in celebration!

Move your candles off the altar and onto the feasting table. Light them and sit around sharing food and stories.

While you share, you are energetically offering thanks to the ancestors.

CHAPTER EIGHT

Embracing Animism Day to Day

A question often asked is: "How to begin or where do I start?" Most people are, in one way or another; animistic.

Developing animism into a practice or sacred devotion takes that basic core belief that is defined in the dictionary as "objects, places and creatures all possessing a distinct spiritual essence.

Animism perceives all things – animals, plants, rocks, rivers, weather systems, human handiwork, and perhaps even words – as animated and alive" to a whole new level.

Unlike organized religions that have detailed 'what-to's' and 'what-not-to's', animism is NOT considered a religion – it's classified as a belief system or way of life. When people ask me what my witchcraft practice is like, I always express that, "It never stops; I eat sleep and breathe this way of life."

When I combine witchcraft with animism, both practices (which are varied and contain different but similar beliefs) end up complimenting each other.

The internet, though vast with information, can often lead people astray and can overwhelm the seeker. While one definition states that animism is not a religion, others that practice it will argue that. For example, another definition clearly states: "Animism is a religious belief that there is a spirit or soul found in objects, places and creatures." The key is not to get caught up in someone else's definition and instead focus on your own.

Most people who practice animism don't often identify themselves as animists. Most are affiliated or align with predominant religions. While I consider myself an animistic witch, it is because of the work I am doing as a witch within the realms of animism. I am also Wiccan and practice Neopaganism; a term for contemporary Nature-centered religions concerned with and focused on the environment. All of what I do in my practice and life takes hold and anchors into animism.

In an article written by Jennifer Waldrep, she states that, "Digging deep uncovers animistic roots in every culture. The West is no exception. The days of the week, Western wedding traditions, and Old Saint Nick are animistic fossils of northern European tribes and clans. Thursday is Thor's Day, and Friday honors the Fertility Goddess Freya. Bridesmaids are decoys meant to confuse malevolent spirits who would snatch the bride away, if only they could see her behind that veil. Father Christmas is less scary than Odin the All Father, who would land his horse-drawn sleigh on the roofs of his worshipers to distribute presents, accompanied by an entourage of ghosts (ever wonder why Hollywood releases ghost stories around Christmastime?)."

Whether we connect the dots together or not, in some way or another most people honor these 'animistic fossils' and are giving them new vigor and life in our modern world.

When asked the questions above, my answer is usually phrased in a question form of "How do you want to begin and when do you want to start?" Not always liked by the students who want everything handed to them, but it's not my question to answer really. I can only give examples and insights of what worked for me and what didn't. Ultimately the one asking the question has to really understand that they will be the one answering it, and how will they answer?

If animism is a strong anchor into the land and all things upon it, then creating a sacred devotion is really quite simple. Stop what you are doing and go outside. Remove your shoes and stand barefoot upon the earth. Close your eyes and focus on your breath. Feel the ground beneath literally holding you up, providing support. Feel the air around you. Is the wind blowing? Is the air hot or is it cold? Now, just for a moment; be fully present. This is a simple practice.

The best way to begin and start is in the present moment. Turn off the distractions of this modern convenient world and engage with the Nature around you. This is what the elevated masters taught.

History is full of culture, pantheons, myths and legends which all anchor into some kind of spirit or source of divinity in all living things. Animism is a deep and sacred devotion and reverence for ALL. Plato called this practice 'anima mundi' or the practice of cultivating a relationship with the world soul.

https://www.imb.org/2018/09/21/do-you-know-the-basics-of-animism/

The belief and practice of animism predates any religion as the very first people to inhabit the land were hunter gatherers and strongly aware of their connection with the land and all that lived upon it. Animism is a simple practice of honoring ALL as divine, whole and sentient. Each animal, plant, rock, tree, fish, parasite and even bacteria, all contain 'anima' – breath, soul or spirit.

One's particular personal practice will determine their connection with the word 'soul' or 'spirit' as they choose to define it. When I go walking in the morning and see the antelope herd that lives in our neighborhood, I offer devotion through song. Just like when I see lizard, snake, spider or even an ant.

These are living, breathing beings that are living on this great giant sphere that I call the Mama, and we are all going about our day to day activities in ways that create a sustaining life. A simple song I sing is "Oh Great ……, I sing to you. I honor you. I bow to you."

Devotion looks different for everyone. Some tribes would share offerings to the land such as sage and tobacco. My offering is song. This is a song I sing to just about everything. It's simple and keeps me in the mindset and focus that ALL things vibrate an energy, soul and spirit – sometimes we just are too distracted to allow for a connection.

Biophilia is defined as: "The innate human instinct to connect with Nature and other living beings." This term comes from psychoanalyst, Erich Fromm, who states that biophilia is "the passionate love of life and of all that is alive." Later, this term was referenced by biologist Edward O. Wilson, who proposed "that the tendency of humans to focus on and to affiliate with Nature and other life-forms has, in part, a genetic basis." Genetic being defined as: "Relating to genes, heredity or origin, or arising from a common origin." Whether biophilia is genetic or not, it is vital! Biophilia has been proven to support and enhance cognitive function, physical health and one's psychological wellbeing.

One's individual relationship with the world and all that lives upon it is life sustaining on so many levels. When I was little, I was taught that all the plants, trees, animals and insects had feelings. I remember throwing a rock once and my mother asking me to consider the feeling of the rock. Did I ask its permission to throw it away from its home?

My youth, like most people, shaped my perspective and the way I interact with the world around me. When one stops and considers if a rock, which most perceive as inanimate or by definition "not alive, showing no signs of life" has feelings, that shifts the view of an inanimate object to now a rock that is alive, animate and actually has feelings.

Not a day goes by that I do not offer gratitude for the way I was raised. Now, as a grandmother, I have a sacred duty and obligation to teach my granddaughter how to view the world. Even though I consider my childhood to have been extraordinary, it is now my time to add to what my childhood may have lacked.

When out harvesting in the garden, I have taught my granddaughter to sing and talk to the plants to offer them energy in exchange for the energy they are providing us. Each day she goes out and sings to her four strawberry plants and, not to be bias, but her strawberries are the sweetest I have ever tasted. I firmly believe it is because the plants know they are being honored as individuals when they are given love and sweetness.

When applied to animals, things shift even more. Teaching children to love, honor and respect all animals creates a world where there will be hopefully less animal abuse and animal consumption.

While I am not advocating becoming a vegan in order to practice animism, as I firmly believe that everyone on this planet has the right to honor their bodies in their own way, I am suggesting that we become more conscious of where our food comes from. Especially when the livestock we raise accounts for more biomass than all humans on earth. Our desire to consume animal products has created damage not just to the planet but to our relationship with animals. If we only see them as a source of food then how can we possibly hope to shift consciousness and start seeing them as family?

It's a worthy rabbit hole to journey down into if one so wishes. So, I have provided a link that will hopefully assist those who are seeking more information:

https://ourworldindata.org/meat-production#livestock-counts

Implementing a more animistic view and approach to life really begins with being mindful and conscious. Consciousness is the art of being aware, sensitive and having a knowledge of one's surroundings. Mindfulness is "a mental state achieved by focusing one's awareness on the present moment, while calmly acknowledging and accepting one's feelings, thoughts, and bodily sensations. Mindfulness is the quality or state of being consciously aware."

One thing that has helped me on my quest and daily journey to be more animistic and present in all things is to honor that I am simply a guest on this planet. I do not own anything. The land is a living entity and therefore cannot be owned by anyone. If this great sphere is goddess or mother, then how can any of us own her? Has she given us consent?

Animals are not ours to own, possess or have dominion over. This goes directly against what the Christian Bible says, in Genesis 1:26, "Let him have dominion over the fish of the sea, and over the birds of the air and over the cattle, and over all the wild animals of the earth, and over every creeping thing that creeps upon the earth."

Dominion is by definition "domain or supreme authority." Did the animals give us, as humans, consent? Permission to own them, dominate them and obtain supreme authority over them?

The problem with this scriptural dogma is that it devalues fish, birds, cattle, all wild animals and all things that creep. It promotes anthropocentrism or, in other words; human supremacy. This act of supremacy promotes violence on the planet. When one establishes ownership over another, they are acting in state of oppression and enforcing outdated patriarchal dichotomies and further displaying unhealthy cycles of objectification.

Mahatma Gandhi stated that "you must be the change you wish to see in the world." What a beautiful statement and ideal, which is more than possible if we just shift our focus. If we can look to Nature as the one with the answers, we can heal our broken society. We can eradicate the poisons of patriarchy upon the planet and move back to a time where we lived as mindful, conscious animists. But this has to start with the individual.

There are many religions and spiritual practices that include animism, from Buddhists, Druids, Wiccans to Pagans, Neopagans and indigenous tribes all over this great sphere we call home. While there are many anthropologists that suggest animism is the root of religion, animism is again not an organized religion – there is no established institution or doctrine.

Animism is influenced by one's culture, landscape and how an individual was raised. In other words (and descriptions), animism varies exponentially. Rituals or sacred ceremonies are one way to practice animism. The indigenous tribal people these rituals were led by were shamans, medicine men/women and/or the witch doctor. Each ritual or ceremony consisted of prayers, songs, dances, offerings and a call to the land and ancestors to assist those circled in ritual. It was a community, clan or tribe collective.

Dr. Daniel Foor spells it out quite simply, "If you look down on people from other backgrounds and see Nature as a resource for humans to exploit, you're not very animist as your relational sphere doesn't extend beyond living humans who are like you. If you appreciate humans of all sorts, connect with companion animals, and respect many wild kin as also intelligent and worthy of respect, then you're more animist. If you also deeply bond with other forms of life and dialogue with plants, animals and other unseen forces, then you are more animist yet. The wider your field of meaningful relationships, the more you fit the description of an animist."

When I am asked what the difference is between Paganism and animism my answer is usually vague as I am not a direct spokesperson for either. I can only offer my own unique point of view, which is that Pagans tend to practice polytheism (many gods) and animists don't really believe in divinity in a source of god/goddess – rather that ALL things are divine. Just like understanding that not all witches are Wiccans, it's safe to say that not all Pagans are animists and not all animists are Pagans.

Living animism is a unique and personal relationship with the world around each individual. No two of us are alike, nor should we strive to be alike. We should honor and respect each other as unique and rare – just like each tree, flower, stone, insect or animal. I am reminded of the song *Colors of the Wind* that Pocahontas sings in the Disney cartoon movie that was released back in 1995, the first time I heard it I got goose bumps or rather 'truth bumps'. This song honors animism and teaches that all things are alive! That "every rock and tree and creature has a life, has a spirit, has a name. The rainstorm and the river are my brothers. The heron and the otter are my friends – and we are all connected to each other." It's one of my favorite Disney songs.

Disney, despite its faults, has given us as humans an anchor and invitation to view the world from an animistic approach. I couldn't say whether or not they are consciously promoting animism but I appreciate it either way.

Just about every one of their movies showcases animals that have names, personalities and feelings. Even *Toy Story* takes inanimate objects, such as a child's plastic toys, and gives them a life; taking them from inanimate to animate. My mother always told me to get to sleep before my toys would wake up. While I am sure she did this so I would go to bed on time, I truly believed that while I was sleeping, my toys and stuffed animals had a life of their own.

My favorite Disney movie is *Brave*, wherein a Scottish princess determines her own fate, within it is woven a broken mother/daughter relationship that is only mended when the mother shapeshifts into a bear. This gives the mother and daughter both an opportunity to view each other differently and to see things from new perspectives.

When I disconnect from the human ego mindset and allow myself to interact with others as if they are all honoring their inner PSA or primary spirit animal, I step into a more animistic way of interacting. In my own relationship with my daughter, I frequently remind myself that her energy is very lion-like and my energy is very wolf-like. New tactics and approaches will make communication easier once I step into this way of living.

It is very animistic to honor other human individuals as their spirit animal. Just like it is animistic to believe that our ancestors are watching over us in the form of animals or trees. Or as 'Father Sky and Mother Moon.' When we cast a circle in ceremony or ritual and call to the guardians of a direction, and call to animals associated with that direction, we are practicing animism.

Another way to incorporate animism is to perform rituals and ceremonies. These are sacred acts of physically moving with intention – raising energy for greater good and allowing each individual to connect with a more meaningful part of themselves. To see oneself as part of something is life-changing.

A ritual or ceremony marks an essential moment, rite of passage, new phase or closing of an old phase and when created hand in hand with Nature, such as performing a ritual to welcome the change in season; it connects us to Nature. We honor the seasonal shifts around us and allow those shifts to be seen as a metaphor or mirror within our own lives.

After all, as humans we are animals and we do move through this world in similar ways with our bear, wolf or raven family. There are times in the cold, dark winter months where we become very tired and desire to sleep more. There are times in the spring where we want to start new projects and have to see things from a bird's eye view in order for those projects to take flight. There are times in the summer when we feel like testing our boundaries and want to explore our surroundings.

We vibrate on this planet in a very similar way with our animal kin, even our plant life. Each time we plant a seed of intention we know that in order for it to grow; we must water and tend to that idea or intent in order for it to reach its full potential.

Realistically, we are all, in one way or another, living an animist lifestyle. We can always do more and should do more! We can all benefit from being more mindful and consciously aware of our part played out on this planet.

EASY STEP BY STEP ACTIVATION OF ANIMISM INTO ONE'S DAY TO DAY

Step 1: Begin Each Day with Gratitude
Thank your bed for holding you as you slept. Thank your blankets for keeping your warm. Thank your lights for resting so that you may also rest. Thank your body, every part of your body! Thank your floor for offering you support. Thank gravity! You get the idea….

Be grateful for everything. An attitude of gratitude develops a habit of being consciously aware and mindful of each aspect of your life and it promotes appreciation for all the little things that you may have taken for granted.

Step 2: Go Outside and Interact with the World
Say good morning to the sky, to the ground, to the plants and all the animals. Birds are typically the first ones to greet the Sun as they rest in the tree tops which are closer to the Sun than we are. So offer a greeting to the birds.

By going outside first thing in the morning, you are consciously interacting with the landscape you live in. It also sets the tone for one's day.

The more time one spends outside interacting with Nature, the more improved one's mental and spiritual health will become.

Step 3: Honor the Animals in your Home
If you have animals, greet them kindly in the morning. Ask them how they slept.

Interact with them as you would another of your human species. See them as not just your equals but your teachers.

Step 4: Honor the Animals in your Day to Day
See each individual you come into contact with, whether that be at home, work, grocery store, on the bus or train etc, as all being animals.

You may not know their PSA (primary spirit animal) but every human individual shares similar traits and characteristics with an animal of the world. When you disconnect from ego mind and enter animism, you open the door to excuse judgment from your day to day.

You don't have to love every animal, plant, rock, insect and so forth, to respect it. Respect is given because they too share this same living space with you and you, as an individual, want to receive respect to, so the best way to achieve that is to give it.

Step 5: Honor the Sustenance that you Consume

Give gratitude and thanks to the water that you drink, the coffee that stimulates you into action in the morning, the tea that heals.

When you acknowledge the food and drink that you put into your body, you step into a more conscious and mindful way of interacting and showing appreciation. Take time to actually taste your food.

When you slow down and honor the food you eat, this promotes a new healthier way of eating because you know what you are putting into your body. You are actually taking time to see it! For example, have you ever sent gratitude to the land that grew the lettuce in your salad?

For those who do eat meat, have you ever thought about where that meat came from? Have you ever thought to give thanks to the animal that gave its life so you can enjoy the hamburger you had for lunch? A shift in perspective really does shift one's life.

Step 6: See How We Are All Connected

We are all divine, whole and sentient beings – just like plants, rocks, insects, animals, mountains, rivers, oceans, micro-organisms, bacteria, and more!

Everything on this planet and the Great Mother Earth herself is alive and vibrating!!! To consciously see this – feel it and know this is to be mindfully conscious of how we are all connected. We are all family. We step into a way of life that is reverent, appreciative, devotional and sacred.

My home is a menagerie of animals. With three dogs, five birds, three turtles, nine chickens and currently five cats; there is never a dull moment. The animals always desire something, whether it is a need that as a human I have agreed to fulfill, or a want. The way my animals communicate with me really isn't that different than the animals I meet and mingle with out in the wild.

In the morning, the first thing I wake up to is the sound of birds singing. Not just our three peace doves and two cockatiels but the birds outside are busy with a chattering of morning bliss. While not everyone is a morning person, which is to be respected, there is much to experience in the early hours of the day when the world is calm (mostly because the television and phone are still in their rest mode from the night before).

As the Sun peaks over the mountain, it seems that everything wakes up! The birds begin their morning tune, the flowers bend and stretch to find the sunbeams and the insects and mammals all begin to greet the day in their own way. This daily wake up routine often reminds me that days are better when greeted with song.

As the Sun reaches its peak height of the day, the bees begin to buzz and their activity increases. The garden itself takes on a whole new life in the afternoon. Sometimes the plants will wilt to express (like the tiny beads of sweat on my forehead) that yes; it is hot at midday! The lizards all come out to bask and do their push-up routine with the Sun blazing upon their tiny scales. The antelope that were all out grazing around coffee time have now found the nearest source of shade and are taking an afternoon nap. Afternoons are a time to be indoors, enjoying a midday nap (just like the dogs) or a time to curl up and read a book. The animals know this and they mirror it.

Then the evening begins to creep in. The bees make their way back to their hives, the lizards retreat and the nighttime animals begin their dance. The owls wake up and begin their hunt. The mice and toads come out of their dens and run about seeking food. The spiders come out to weave their webs. It's interesting that most artists experience creativity surges in the late hours of the evening and early hours of the morning. Just like spider.

We, as animals have our routines. Some of us are up ready to sing in the morning. Others are slow moving and prefer the nightlife, while others reach their peak in the middle of the day. Regardless, there is always an animal that we can relate to – that we can look to – that is most likely already there just trying to get our attention and help us see within that particular mirror.

The best way to live an animistic life is to be conscious. When you see an animal, stop and enjoy the moment. Allow a connection. Be open to a connection. Maybe the lizard you meet on your walk one day will be a beacon of transformation and offer you permission to bask in the sunshine of your life? Maybe that songbird will stop singing its morning tune and offer you a cry of alert – something so out of character that you take notice – and maybe, just maybe, that alert cry will get you to pay attention and listen to your gut more?

When you look to all animals as sacred teachers, you open yourself up to receive their messages. You are, after all, the one that will take the time to internalize and contemplate if your chance encounter was really just chance.

So, be open. Allow the animals to speak to you. Allow yourself to be humble and bow to the masters in sacred devotion. Whether they be of padded paws, hoofed, taloned, clawed, finned, scaled, feathered, furry or slimy. Whether they bark, howl, hiss, yip, caw, grunt or neigh. Animals have so much to offer us if we remember that we do NOT have dominion over this land or the animals.

We are guests here on this great sphere some of us call 'the mama' – the animals are our sisters and brothers. We could be more gracious guests. Leave no trace behind. Walk upon the earth with grace and be gentle with each step so as to not make too large of a footprint for the next generation to fill in. We could stop killing animals and eating animals. Or, if meat is a necessity, we could offer more gratitude and be aware of where the meat source comes from. We could simply be more mindful – we could certainly be more conscious.

CHAPTER NINE

Animals you May Encounter as you Turn the Wheel

There are so many animals with so many incredible messages. This chapter is just a sampling of a few animals that I have had the pleasure of working with, either in their animal form or in the form of humans mirroring back to me their PSA (primary spirit animal).

When we attach an animal to the people in our life it really does open up our perspective and allow for honest interactions free from ego.

BREATHING INTO BEAR MIND

Every human being on the planet has access to their imagination. Some of us have lost connection with our childlike mind through struggles, trauma and the hustle and bustle of being adults. But we all have the ability to access, to awaken and step into our bear mind through visualization.

Remember when you were little and you would 'make believe' as animals? Well, this is not an art that is lost to us. We can still play and pretend.

In this book, we will call it "activate and visualize with our mind's eye". Christopher Penczak has said many times, "If you seek to know the witch's way, ever mind the child of play." Children, like animals, are the greatest teachers and we need to look to them for that knowing of how to live purely in this world.

As a grandmother, I am spoiled because my granddaughter, who is two, lives with me. My home has become a child's world and, as such, my goal is to help her create and feed her imagination constantly. In our home, she is our center and when she wants to be a baby bear we all play along. Only, I never really get to be a bear because she knows I work with wolves, so I am always 'Gigi Wolf' who gets to play with baby bear and her 'Papa Bear'.

What I am emphasizing is that you are never too old to play. When you can get down on the ground and really move your body and visualize yourself as an animal, it will help with your shapeshifting capabilities.

Let's move into your mind's eye with a little exercise. This exercise can be used with the yoga pose below.

> Close your eyes and disconnect from this realm. Let go of your thoughts, disconnect from ego and activate the present moment by focusing on your breath.
>
> Let your muscles relax as you move through breath work.
>
> Inhale to the count of five and exhale to the count of five. It is optional to hold your breath for five counts between each inhale and exhale. You may feel the desire to slightly open your mouth as you exhale out and make sound, a grunt, low soft growl or an accentuated exhale. When we exhale, we release stress, wandering thoughts, toxins and tension. So, really make the most of your exhales.
>
> **(repeat this breath work five times)**
>
> In your mind's eye, visualize your physical body as that of a bear.
>
> Allow an extra layer of thick rubbery-like skin to wrap around you, creating insulation, warmth and protection. Allow your hands and feet to become thick padded paws with sharp curved claws at the tips of each finger and toe. Visualize your entire body being covered with thick fur.
>
> Breathe in nice and deep with your bear nose.
>
> Open your ears to hear more clearly with your bear ears.
>
> Give yourself permission to simply sit here as a bear. Large in statue. Calm in the knowing of your inner and outer strength. Just sit. Breathe into your bear mind. Awaken the bear within.
>
> What does your bear want? Are you in need of strength? Calm? Protection?
>
> When you are ready, open your bear eyes and see your surroundings.
>
> **(pause)**
>
> Closing your eyes once more, breathe down deep and low, all the way to your padded paws.

If you feel like moving into a different physical form, trust your inner bear to guide you.

Give yourself time here as bear. When you are ready, simply visualize shedding your fur, removing your padded paws and claws, and taking off the thick layer of rubbery skin. Allow your physical body to slowly move. Wiggle your fingers and your toes. You may want to touch your arms and legs, your face. Breathe back into you. Knowing you can access bear any time you wish.

JOURNAL PROMPT

How was your breath work activation with bear? What kind of bear were you?

PHYSICAL EMBODIMENT OF MOTHER BEAR THROUGH YOGA OR MERUDANDASANA

Moving your body into a physical pose such as the bear pose below will help in visualizing and activating more depth into your connection with bear. This is a calming pose designed to help open up your hips, and enhance flexibility and balance.

Begin in butterfly position; seated with the soles of the feet together. Next, grasp your big toes with your middle and index fingers. Shift your weight to your tailbone, lean back and straighten your legs out into a V shape. Hold this pose for six to eight breaths.

While you breathe, visualize yourself as a calm mother bear. Breathe into your bear mind.

HONORING BEAR AS DIVINE MASCULINE STRENGTH

Just as with Mother Bear, who brings calm, nurturing and gentle protection, it is important to honor the opposite as that will create a space of balance.

Masculine and feminine attributes are not solely anchored into gender or the physical.

We all possess some attributes that are more feminine and we all possess others that are more masculine – but these have nothing to do with gender specifics – as we are beings of energy, not bound by our physical bodies.

There are times in our lives where we need to be gentle and nurturing and there are times when we need to be wild, untamed and become a warrior for ourselves and/or others.

There are times when we need to be Bear Mother and provide soothing love and there are times when we need to be a fierce berserker and fight. Understanding time and place is vital to bringing both bears within; into balance.

If you or partner have become acquainted with the solitary male berserker bear, how can you offer a space for them that will allow this wildness to surface (within reason of course)?

Oftentimes, bear people who are more connected with the solitary male bear in meditation are in need of their own space and time to process things. Again, the importance of having one's own cave or room is vital in providing them solitary time. Bear people can have the tendency towards outbursts of growling, or temper tantrums – these must be allowed to be expressed, but in a healthy way.

Bear people need to wander so, when emotions arise, is it possible to take a time out and let emotions cool before moving towards a resolution conversation? As wolf, this is hard for me as my lover is very much connected to the solitary masculine bear, and when I want to talk and work through disagreements; he does not. If I push the matter then tensions build and growling will ultimately occur. So, pushing the 'pause button' is a good technique. I am not excusing irrational outbursts as being okay in any way. However, we all have a tendency towards anger and frustrations can build up. Walking or going on a journey is very useful, regardless of what bear you are honoring as your mirror.

Another tip I have found with bear is, again, patience. Sometimes bear people hide behind their thick layer and process things internally. An outlet for physical release is very helpful. Again; walking!

The bear people in our lives will thrive if they are given space and patience. There will be times in all of our lives where we need space to process and patience to follow through at our own pace.

Seeing the bear in each other can be overwhelming but I have found there to be great calm and protection when bear comes into our lives.

PHYSICAL EMBODIMENT OF BERSERKER BEAR

The berserkers were warriors who were said to have fought in a trance-like state while wearing the hide of a bear or becoming bears themselves. The term 'berserker' means *bear shirt*. The definition of berserk is: "1–an ancient Scandinavian warrior frenzied in battle and held to be invulnerable; 2–one whose actions are recklessly defiant." Other definitions include: "3–crazed Norse warriors who fought in frenzy; 4–injuriously, maniacally or furiously violent and out of control."

These bear warriors were said to have fought side by side with *heathen wolves* – fierce warriors (wearing wolf pelts) who would harness the powers of wolves and, together, they formed a frightening attacking force on those they battled.

They would howl, growl and behave erratically while in attack mode and afterwards they were said to be physically weak. This is shapeshifting taken to a whole new level! Some believed the berserkers and wolfskins to have consumed psychoactive substances such as hallucinogenic fly agaric mushrooms (*amanita muscaria*) or large amounts of alcohol that gave them the power to physically shift into these great wild animals and made them almost invincible. What gave them additional power was their belief that they really were these animals. There was no separation between the man and the beast – they became one!

The oldest written description of berserkers comes from a ninth century Skaldic poem that honored King Harald. It states; "Berserkers roared where the battle raged, wolf-heathens howled and iron weapons trembled."

In Grettir's saga (1914 translation into English taken from the original Icelandic 'Grettis saga') of the Battle of Hafrsfjord between King Harald and Thorir 'Long-Chin', who was said to be a terrible berserker, "ordered his berserks, the men called wolfskins, forward. No iron could hurt them, and when they charged nothing could withstand them."

Just imagine a group of warriors, no armor, wearing only the hide of bears and wolves charging towards you in battle in a frenzy, so wild and untamed that they appear to no longer be men but animals. That would be a very frightening site!

Some scholars believe them to be warrior shamans who could only possess these predator aspects through intense rituals that included living isolated in the wilderness, starving themselves, exposing themselves to extremes of hot and cold and adopting the mannerisms and habits of bears and wolves.

"This fury, which was called *berserkergang*, occurred not only in the heat of battle, but also during laborious work. Men who were thus seized performed things which otherwise seemed impossible for human power. This condition is said to have begun with shivering, chattering of the teeth, and chill in the body, and then the face swelled and changed its color. With this was connected a great hot-headedness, which at last gave over into a great rage, under which they howled as wild animals, bit the edge of their shields, and cut down everything they met without discriminating between friend or foe.... A demoniacal frenzy suddenly took him; he furiously bit and devoured the edges of his shield; he kept gulping down fiery coals; he snatched live embers in his mouth and let them pass down into his entrails; he rushed through the perils of crackling fires; and at last, when he had raved through every sort of madness, he turned his sword with raging hand against the hearts of six of his champions. It is doubtful whether this madness came from thirst for battle or natural ferocity."

These warriors had one goal, and that was to become the bear or wolf. To go 'berserk' was to *hamask* which translates as 'change form' – shapeshifting!

It should be noted that in 1015, Norway officially outlawed this cult of Odin, referred to as berserkers. There are many myths, legends and sagas that mention berserkers, such as Grendel in *Beowulf*, who fought with a frenzy of a wild animal and fitful rage – after which he fell into extreme exhaustion.

In stories of werewolves, it is mentioned that after the shift from man to wolf and back to man, the physical body is in what appears to be a near death exhaustion. An incredible book on werewolves and shapeshifting is *Werewolf Magick* by Denny Sargent. I read it in one sitting and will read it over and over again. What a powerful breakdown of werewolves through history and it proves that all people possess the innate ability to connect with animals through observation, intention, invocation and ritual.

Through physical movement, you can build physical strength, which will increase confidence. A bear crawl is an intense core-building exercise that also strengthens your shoulders and legs.

To move into bear crawl, begin by placing your hands and knees flat on the ground, coming into table top yoga pose – keep your back flat and your legs hip width apart. Come up onto your toes, keeping your knees bent in a 90 degree angle. Slowly begin to move one hand and the opposite foot forward, keeping your body low to the ground. Begin to crawl.

Really accentuate your movements and remember to stay low to the ground. This exercise is best done with your breath being focused. You can access bear mind in this pose by growling or grunting on each exhale.

BONUS BEAR CONNECTION

If you find yourself to be ill, or hurting and feeling alone and isolated, one thing you can do is lay down on your bed or floor, close your eyes and visualize a great big, warm, fuzzy bear wrapping themselves around you. Holding you. Giving you its warmth and a protected space to honor your feelings. Allow bear to come through with a warm 'bear hug'.

Oftentimes, when I do long distance reiki for clients who are ill or experiencing sorrow, I will visualize a great bear holding them. Saying nothing – for bears are not big at vocalizing – but simply holding them. Offering them that silent protective strength.

WELCOMING THE MOTHER BEAR

When I travel and offer animal connection meditations, it is always fascinating to me who connects with bear. For some, a very masculine bear comes through, and for others a very female mama bear which comes through. There is definitely a reason for this.

My father is very much the man of the house; he is wise, works hard and has always taken excellent care of our family.

When I was invited to share my animal connection meditation at a family reunion, I was not at all surprised that my father met a very fierce and protective grizzly bear as his mirror. Two years later, at another family reunion, I was asked once again to take everyone through the meditation and my father saw a mama bear with cubs.

There has been a shift in my father as everyone has gotten older and the grandkids have grown. We are no longer in need of a fierce protector and he no longer needs to be the solitary papa bear. He truly has embodied the essence of a mama bear – he is calm, nurturing and devoted to seeing that his children, grandchildren and great-grandchild are cared for.

If bear shows up as your primary mirror or as a mirror for someone you are engaged with in a personal or intimate relationship, it is important to allow them their own space, their own den or bear cave. Bears are solitary animals and their hibernation period can symbolize the need to go within and do some soul work or soul-itary work. After all, bears are considered shamans.

European and Native American shamans recognize bears as being a source of strength to activate and awaken the unconscious. Bears are known as the great healers. European and Native Americans also recognize shamans to be a source of strength to activate the unconscious. Shamans too are known as great healers. Can you see the healer within you?

By definition, a shaman is someone who acts as a bridge between the shamanic indigenous world and the modern world. I am no shaman, nor do I claim to be, but as a priestess and constant student of life and all its many lessons, I am often a bridge. By helping connect clients to their animal mirror, I am simply acting as a bridge – their subconscious does all the work.

They choose to embrace the meditative experience and they choose as individuals to honor the authentic connection with whatever animal shows up. I simply provide the words and then after the meditation I share the tips and techniques that I have found to be helpful. In a way, I embody bear as the mother archetype.

As parents, we can offer many lessons to our children but they are the ones that choose to implement what they learn. I once asked my father for some fatherly advice concerning how to be a good mother to my adult children who were not making the best of life choices, and his words have stuck with me since: "You can lead a horse to water but you can't make it drink."

Your decision to embrace bear as mirror is completely up to you. Just like any animal that shows up as a teacher, messenger or guide – it is up to you, the reader, to engage and consciously make an effort to connect and allow yourself to honor the teachings that each animal has to offer or not.

With bear – are you in need of protection? Or are you in need of stepping into confidence and seeing your strength? Are you ready to sit with yourself inside your den and do some inner soul workings? Are you in need of a hibernation period? A journey?

BREATHING INTO HARE MIND

This meditation is best done outside on the grass on a nice spring day:

THE WHEEL OF THE YEAR

Sitting upon the earth, settle into a comfortable physical position. Allow your body to rest upon the earth, either sitting or lying down. Mentally move through the inventory of your body, beginning with your head and moving all the way down to your toes and, as you do so, consciously release any tension within your body. Once your body is relaxed, close your eyes and focus on your breath.

Take a nice slow, precise and conscious inhale to the count of four and exhale to the count of four.

Continue this breathing pattern for five repetitions. In your mind's eye, your home of imagination and your inner sight, see yourself burrowed into a soft patch of leaves, grass and fur under a small shrub.

Feel the warmth and protection that this tiny nest upon earth gives you. Feel yourself curled up like a hare, all tucked in nice and cozy. Around you, the forest is beginning to wake up as spring has finally arrived. The animals nearby are actively waking up, the birds are chatting amongst themselves, the tiny blossoms of spring are opening and stretching towards the Sun that is basking everyone in a pleasant heat of a new day. As hare, you begin to stretch, moving your tiny front paws up to your face you rub your face as if to wake it up. You stretch up moving your paws up and down, your large ears are keenly listening to the sounds of spring. Your large hind legs and feet begin to move and you sit ready to hop. An overwhelming sense of excitement fills you up and you take that first hop of the day out of your nest and begin to run and hop through the forest. It is as if you are greeting everyone else who has awakened on this most perfect first day of spring. You leap, hop, jump and sprint in a most unpredictable and wild manner without a care in the world. When you finally come to a stop, you extend your ears up even higher, listening to any messages that may be blowing in the wind or coming from nearby animals. Your hare eyes see clearly all the fine details of your surroundings and you breathe in nice and slow as you honor each of your incredible senses. Here in hare form, you can be calm, gentle and serene or you can be enraptured, alive and somewhat hysterical. Hare medicine and magick comes from the unknown hidden depths within that stimulate you to awaken and do things that you normally wouldn't do. So, for just a few moments, be a mad like the hares in spring.

(pause)

Now that you have frolicked in the forest, it is time to readjust to your current human surroundings.

See yourself moving back to your cozy nest and cuddle up. Feel your fur becoming skin, your paws becoming feet and hands, feel your essence of human take shape as you shift from hare to person.

When you are ready, open your eyes, stretch your legs and arms, move your fingers and toes and activate your physical body into this present moment.

JOURNAL PROMPT

Take a few moments to write down anything that made an impression during your meditation. How did it feel to connect with the instincts of hare?

How did it feel to embrace to season of spring?

HONORING SALMON ATTRIBUTES

Salmon essence and energy is primarily based upon a strong desire to complete a task at hand. These incredible creatures persevere, which by definition means: "persistence in doing something despite difficulty or delay in achieving success."

How one activates perseverance in each task or journey at hand is just one way to define one's character. Are you willing to put in the effort to achieve something despite it being difficult? Can you face and honor moments of failure and opposition as teaching lessons, or will you drown in those depths? Can you be steadfast?

Determination, instinct, accuracy and precision are all qualities to be admired in those who activate salmon essence in their lives. Think of all the people you admire, people who have struggled, worked hard, kept going despite the challenges. Isn't it possible to consider that you too contain within you everything you need to have similar achievements?

When I first began my journey into Paganism as an anchor and way of life, what I first felt inspired by was the self-accountability. My success was determined by me. This is true for everyone regardless of what you anchor into. At the end of the day, you face yourself within the mirror. When all's said and done; you answer to you. Did you make the most of your day?

Did you face some obstacles along the way? Are you willing to learn from those or are you going to wallow for a bit?

Salmon energy, essence, medicine and magick are all about the determination to continue, to keep on going despite not always knowing the end outcome. Keep going and know that you may not achieve everything in one day. But you have to keep going!

When honoring or activating salmon medicine and magick within yourself, it is important to focus on one task, challenge or goal at a time. Some of us love to multitask and take on too much! This can be overwhelming at times and when overwhelmed our species (human) has a tendency to quit – to give up and to lose motivation.

Too much piled onto any plate can and eventually does cause the plate to crack! Keep things simple. Narrow things down and prioritize.

TIPS TO NARROW THINGS DOWN

They say in witchcraft, that to succeed, all one needs is intention. While this is good in theory, one can never truly succeed without following through. Remember back in the late 90's early 2000 when affirmations were the big thing? Well, stating an "I am..." affirmation can be helpful in shifting one's perspective, the key really is to follow through. One can say over and over, a thousand times each day: "I am a money magnet," but that won't ensure that money will simply fall from the sky.

In order to be financially successful, one must get out and do some work. Put some time, energy and intention into creating one's financial success.

The same goes for activating salmon medicine and magick. One has to be willing to not only set the intention but create actions that will follow through and give life to one's intent. Keeping things simple and narrowing things down a bit helps tremendously in avoiding burn out.

Make a list! Write down three things that you are currently working on, facing or about to embrace through activation. With this list of three things, categorize them based upon your priority.

Which one comes first? Now, next to each of these three, write down three things you can do to start giving them energy.

For Example
1. Regain health:
   a. cut back on foods that weaken immune system
   b. drink more water
   c. take vitamins
2. Lose weight:
   a. walk every day
   b. eat smaller, healthier meals
   c. join a gym
3. Meditate more:
   a. dedicate five minutes each day to creating a meditation practice
   b. sit and focus on breathing five minutes a day
   c. download a meditation app

This is an easy way to narrow things down and prioritize things.

When you focus on just a small amount of tasks, and cross off each thing as you accomplish it, you can clearly see just how much determination and perseverance you really have.

This form of list making can be applied to any aspect of your life.

Give yourself some credit and remember you can be like salmon and swim against the current to make your intentions come to life!

I always recommend that you place your list somewhere in your home or on your altar where you can see it every day and remind yourself of what you are working on. Time and energy is an investment into yourself. You are worthy of investing in!

PUTTING IT ALL TOGETHER

Go back to your intention list. You may want to activate these intentions in ritual space. To do so, create your container. Cast a circle, say a prayer, light a candle or, if you prefer, go to a natural body of water. Take your list and spend some time honoring the intentions you have set. You may want to inscribe the Vegvisir upon your list.

With your list in your hand, close your eyes and breathe into salmon mindset. Focus mentally on all that you are willing to do to honor these intentions and see yourself working through each step and, as you do so, feel the sense of accomplishment that naturally will occur once you see these intentions come to life and later fulfilled.

Ritual or ceremony is a very personal activation and commitment with yourself however you, as the individual, choose to define the divine. If you are wanting to move swiftly and away from something, you may feel inclined to call upon Loki to help you shift. If you are wanting to obtain knowledge and wisdom in this process of working through each intention, you may want to call upon the Great Salmon of Knowledge. Or, if you have the desire to honor and respect salmon attributes and qualities within yourself, you could take inventory of how salmon has inspired and sustained you and will provide for you.

The key is to make this ritual experience unique to you, as you are the practitioner of your magick. The connection you choose to embrace in salmon is merely a reflection of the attributes you are choosing to embrace within yourself.

HOW CAN YOU HONOR THE SALMON PEOPLE IN YOUR LIFE?

When we begin to lose the socially projected patriarchal mindset of competition, we can begin to see everyone that we come into contact with as a teacher, messenger and guide.

Seeing the people in our life that share similar characteristics and attributes with salmon can be inspiring. For example, there are people in all of our lives that work incredibly hard to achieve the impossible. What if, instead of looking at them with envy or a little resentment for their successes, we see them as an inspiration? Can we disconnect from competition and embrace honor and respect?

Do you have salmon people in your life that defy all odds? Salmon people have the tendency to be flexible and adapt rather than resist. If the only thing constant in our lives is change, then adapting to what is happening around us, rather than resisting it, will create growth.

Of course, all things within reason. Salmon live in both fresh water and salt water. We too can learn to thrive in different environments.

Do you trust your instincts and use your common sense? There is a saying that "common sense is not so common." Well, if you are activating your instincts, then you will know that hot water burns and you do not have to put your finger in the pot to test this theory.

This goes with certain situations as well, if you know within that the road up ahead is going to be painful and bestow heartache; trust your gut and don't pursue that path.

Be prepared for the journey ahead. No matter where you go in life, whether it is work or on an ancestral pilgrimage, pack light! Salmon do not eat the entire time they journey from the sea back to their birthplace.

Maybe it's time to do an inventory of the baggage you emotionally carry around and hold onto? What if you could keep work issues at work and not bring them home? The same can be applied to just about any issue one chooses to hold onto.

Whatever you decide to do in life – don't give up!

Just like Dori in *Finding Nemo*; just keep swimming! Some waters in life will be choppy and others will be calm. Enjoy the journey as you swim.

MEDITATION TO HELP YOU STAY CALM IN THE WATERS OF LIFE

Move into a relaxed physical position and focus once more on your breath.

Taking a nice slow deep inhale to the count of four and exhale to the count of four.

Repeat this breath pattern until you feel your body releasing all physical tension and your mind becomes clear and focused. In your intuitive mind, see yourself floating in a calm stream.

Feel the waters hold you and support you as you simply float with the current.

These waters represent the waters of your life. For this moment allow those waters to be calm.

Allow the waters to move you further down the stream.

In this state, you are simply allowing. You are not actively engaged in whatever issues you may currently be facing – you are present in this here and now.

This calm state is an energetic pause.

There are times in life where we all must swim in choppy waves and there are times when we float.

For this moment – float! Enjoy the peace that comes with surrender.

(pause)

Now see behind you a challenge or task that you are currently facing. See it for what it is.

When you are ready, in your mind's eye, see your body begin to shift, see scales and fins appearing. Move into salmon mind and begin to swim.

Breathe into your inner salmon and activate determination, confidence and perseverance.

Move in the water with precision and begin to swim upstream towards this challenge or task that lies ahead in the waters. Push through the currents, move past the stones and boulders.

Keep going! Don't give up.... Swim faster! Swim harder!

Allow your tail fins to propel you through the rough rapids that are ahead.

Be the salmon!

JOURNAL PROMPT

Take some time to write down how it felt to just be held by water. When we write things down, we activate them into a conscious state and we give them life. So, be specific.

What did you feel as you simply floated in the water? What challenges or tasks were upstream? How will you swim confidently towards them? How will you activate salmon medicine and magick to conquer these?

ANIMALS YOU MAY ENCOUNTER AS YOU TURN THE WHEEL

PRONGHORN ANTELOPES – KEEPERS OF CROSSROADS

Here in Utah we have pronghorn antelopes. These majestic creatures live in small herds. In our local herd, which wanders my neighborhood, we have eight in the herd. We have what I fondly call the 'Papa' who is very stoic and protective of his family. Currently there are four new babies that have joined the herd this year.

Each morning, on my walk, I see them. Some are just the mothers with their young and very rarely I see just the Papa walking solo. I know he is never alone and that he has the rest of the herd somewhere safe and he is standing guard.

Pronghorn antelopes are the fastest mammal in North America! They can reach speeds of up to 70 mph. This brings them into second place of the world's fastest land mammals, after the cheetah! They are native to our area and are referred to as 'crepuscular', which is a fancy word that means being most active at dawn and dusk. Their diet consists of sagebrush, which we have an ample amount of where we live.

Pronghorn antelopes have very large round eyes which allow them 300 degrees of vision. This is eight times that of a human's sight. They are a species of *'antilocapridae'* and the pronghorns are the only one of their species still alive today. The species known as antelopes belong to the *'Bovidae'* species, alongside gazelles, impalas, cattle and sheep. This makes the pronghorn antelope unique and extremely sacred. The nearest living relative to the pronghorn antelope is actually the giraffe.

Why are pronghorns referred to as antelopes if they are not in fact antelopes? Well, it's simply because they resemble antelopes. A female is called a doe and the male is called a buck. They both can grow horns but the females' only reach a few inches while the males' horns can reach up to twelve inches. The males also have a black patch under their neck, almost like a neckband, which helps them to stand apart.

Their horns (which are not shed like deer horns – ie. each season) are considered a *true horn*, in the sense that they are derived from hair, not antlers. The horns have an outer sheath of fused, modified hair that covers a bony core. The horns are considered sacred and have been used by many different cultures for medicinal and magical purposes.

In the realm of animal messengers, horns and antlers represent heightened intelligence, activation and connection with the divine and are a source of higher spiritual wisdom. This is due to the locations at which they sit, which is the brow and crown chakras.

MAGICAL ATTRIBUTES OF THE PRONGHORN ANTELOPE

Intelligence. Wisdom. Focus. Protection. Vigor. Vision. Instinctual. Adaptable. Focus. Perception. Alert. Watchful. Centered.

KEEPERS OF THE CROSSROADS

One day I was pulling out of my driveway and heading into town, which is about a fifteen minute drive. I was angry and in flight mode, following an argument. My reaction instinct was to just leave. I made it about three quarters of a mile down my dirt road when I came to the crossroad where the road split. In the center was sitting a herd of antelopes. Sitting! They saw my approaching car and did not move. In fact, when I got within five feet of them, they still would not move. I even got out of my car and they just stared at me. So I got in my car, backed up and went home.

Pronghorn antelopes will always represent pathways and crossroads. They are very instinctual and alert animals – sensing danger with their keen eyesight, sense of smell and pure gut response. These pronghorns knew that I meant them no harm but I firmly believe that, had I kept going that day, things in my life would have gotten exponentially worse.

These incredible animals are masters of intuition and instinct. They are loyal and, like a wolf pack, they are very protective. Each antelope within the herd is of sacred importance. Each spring the female will give birth in a totally new location each year as a protection strategy.

Antelopes are survivalists! They can go years without drinking water and this is largely due to their incredibly complex digestive systems that enable them to acquire all the water they need from the plants they eat. They teach us to adapt and make the most of our current situations and environment.

If pronghorn antelopes show themselves to you – take notice. Sit with their message. Are they in alert mode? Are their ears perked as if to advise you to listen carefully? Are their eyes focused on something specific? What are they asking you to see with more depth? Like deer, antelopes are messengers of the senses. They are telling us to pay attention! What are you smelling? Is it ill intent or flower gardens? Trust your gut is what the pronghorn shows.

Just yesterday, I was out on my morning walk and not really paying attention to my surroundings. I was talking out loud to myself and going over an upcoming public speaking engagement, when I heard a strange almost hiss-like sound. I was startled, stopped where I stood and looked to my left to see that I had interrupted the local pronghorn herd's morning. They were literally within ten feet of me. With sacred devotion, I apologized and sang to them as I slowly walked the other way. The message I absorbed from this encounter was: *"Tread lightly upon this earth, protect your family and let the little ones lead the way."*

We have so much to learn from animals if we just observe. When I interrupted this herd, they all moved to protect the little ones. In fact, the four babies ran in the opposite direction of me whilst the mothers followed behind. The 'Papa' gave me a stern gaze which let me know that I was to pay better attention in future.

Pronghorn antelopes are often linked to being elegant, graceful and docile – they mirror to us, as humans, how we should honor the sacred and vital connection that we have personally with the land.

Do we stomp about as if we disrespect this land or as if we own it? Or do we walk softly as if we respect each bit of earth that we are blessed enough to walk upon? Are we quick to flee from harmful situations or do we rush in with arrogance and ego? Are we using our intelligence and senses?

MEDITATION CONNECTION WITH PRONGHORN ANTELOPES

If possible, do this meditation at an actual crossroad. One way to accomplish that is to go out in Nature and draw or create a large circle on the ground and in the center create a crossroad.

Think of four things in your life that you are currently facing and link those four things to each pathway of the crossroad.

Close your eyes and enter a meditative state.

Focus on your breath and allow your physical body to relax and release any stress or tension.

Breathing in to the count of four and exhaling to the count of four.

Repeat until your body is relaxed and your mind is open.

Here in this state, see before you the crossroad you have created or visualize one in your mind's eye. See that this crossroad represents current choices or pathways in your life and that you are in need of choosing which path is of priority, the one which you are soulfully ready to walk down.

See before you a large pronghorn antelope buck standing in the center of the crossroad.

He stands tall and is very seriously looking at you – his gaze penetrating into your psyche.

He is challenging you to see with a new perspective. His ears are perked and he looks at each pathway as if to ask you: "Have you listened to the messages attached to each pathway?"

Now see his nostrils – how they flare open and closed.

He is showing you to trust your gut, activate your instincts and sniff it out.

Out of these four things you are currently facing in your life, you can safely eliminate one.

You will know which one is of least importance.

Observe how the crossroad has narrowed down to three choices. Three options. Three pathways.

When you are ready, and feel connected with pronghorn as sacred teacher, ask this majestic buck to show you which path to walk down. Then wait. Let him show you the way. Do not fight or argue.

Do not embrace ego mind and start weighing the pros and cons.

Once antelope has picked a pathway – get up and follow.

JOURNAL PROMPT

Take some time to journal about your meditation with pronghorn antelope.

What senses did you find easier to tap into? What senses did you and do you resist trusting? Which pathway did you choose and how can you keep moving down this pathway with confidence?

Oftentimes in life we procrastinate and resist the inevitable. Instead of just moving forward one step at a time, we prolong things by second-guessing them or talking ourselves out of taking on a particular task that we know we will have to deal with eventually anyway. Pronghorns are masters of survival.

Trust that, no matter what, you will be able to adapt, seek out what you need to assist you on your task and see that staying stagnant is no longer an option.

JACKAL MEDICINE AND MAGICK

In the rather large family of the canines, you have many relatives – from coyote, wolf, fox to dog and jackal. What's the difference? Well, really there isn't much of a physical difference rather it is a location factor. In North America, we have coyote and wolf. Jackals primarily live in Africa, some parts of Europe and Asia.

There are four species of jackal – the golden or most common jackal, the side striped jackal and the black back jackal, with the coyote also being considered a jackal. Think of a German shepherd mixed with a fox and you get the idea of what a jackal looks like.

Unlike their relative, the wolf, jackals are not pack-oriented – at least, not all of them. Some species are very social and live in packs of about six, while others are solitary. When in a pair, they are monogamous and do everything together. Jackals are similar to pronghorn antelopes in that they prefer the dawn and dusk hours of the day – with the exception of the side striped jackal, which is nocturnal.

You may be wandering why not just focus on wolf or coyote? In my travels of offering animal readings to individuals, jackal has actually shown up more than coyote. In my first book, I devoted an entire chapter to both wolf and coyote; now it's time to give jackal the spotlight.

JACKAL IN MYTH AND LEGEND

When you hear 'jackal' there is almost always one God that comes to mind and that is Anubis. It is Anubis who weighed the hearts of the decedents on one scale and a feather on the other. It was Anubis who presided over the embalming process and walked with the dead as companion into the afterworld, making him God or Gatekeeper of the Underworld and 'Conductor of Souls.'

Anubis is a masculine deity depicted with the head of a jackal. He is the son of Osiris and Nephthys. There are other jackal gods in ancient Egypt such as Wepwawet and Duamutef. The jackal gods of ancient Egypt were nearly all males. It is Anubis that one meets to measure the impact of their life after they die to determine whether or not they will enter the Underworld. Anubis is said to be the one who created the art of embalming – an art that he first performed on Osiris.

With gratitude to Neil Gaiman and his book *American Gods*, we are seeing depicted on television the old gods in a modern world. In season two of the television series you meet Mr Jacquel (no coincidence on the name) as Anubis, who runs a funeral parlor with his partner Mr Ibis, who is a depiction of the ancient Egyptian God Thoth.

Whether these depictions are historically accurate or not, they are creating a resurgence and appreciation for the old gods which is really quite incredible.

MANY NAMES AND TITLES OF ANUBIS

Master of Secrets. He who is in the Place of Embalming. Gatekeeper of the Underworld. Lord of Sacred Land. He who is Upon his Sacred Mountain. Old One. He who Protects the Dead. Foremost of the Divine Booth. Ruler of the Nine Bows. The Dog who Swallows Millions. Lord of the Dead.

ATTRIBUTES OF JACKALS

Being nocturnal creatures and animals that seek out the dawn and dusk, jackals are often associated with the occult, sorcery and witchcraft. The jackal is linked to death, new beginnings and rebirth. They are scavengers and, similar to coyote, they are known as tricksters.

With jackals being both known to be loyal and devoted companions to their mates, or being solitary, they are often associated with dualities. In relationships, jackals may appear to show that there needs to be time for solitary time and as a mirror of how strong the relationship is.

It helps tremendously when each person in a relationship has their own space, their own needs, their own dreams, desires and can come together collectively as loyal and devoted.

Jackals, like the pronghorn antelopes, are survivors. They will adapt! Jackals are cunning and wise – rulers of strategy. If you combine the polarities of loyalty with solitary, the mysteries of the occult and the intelligence needed to survive; you have the essence of jackals. Now, how can you apply those lessons to your life?

THE NOT SO POSITIVE SIDE OF JACKAL

Rather than viewing jackal as an omen of Anubis coming, and death on its way, what if you saw jackal as a messenger of challenge? Not a challenge that one dwells and runs in fear from, but a challenge that stimulates confidence and expansion.

When I think of the connection between Anubis and jackal, I think of the measure of one's life. In the ancient texts it states that: "Upon one's death they will meet Anubis who will hold two scales. On one scale he will weigh the heart of the deceased and on the other a feather that represents the Goddess Ma'at, she of truth and judgment. If the heart weighs more than the feather then the person would either be fed to the monster Ammut, who is both hippo and lion, or they would go into the Underworld. If the heart was lighter than the feather, the person would ascend to the afterlife. This lightness of heart has to do with the measure of one's life amongst the living. If a person's heart was light, they had done many good deeds free of sin, making them pure of heart."

How would you measure your life? Have you lived with pure heart and intent?

Looking to animals as messengers, one must dig a bit deeper for meaning and lessons. This digging deep means analyzing one's own life. Jackal tends to show up when it's time to take inventory.

Look to your ancestors and ask yourself if their heart was lighter or heavier than the feather? Do you strive to be the best you can be each day? And if you do, are you doing that for the greater good or for self-elevation? And is that self-elevation at the expense of others?

This style of questioning can be applied to one's occult or solitary practice within the Craft. Are you pursuing the craft for self gain or are you actively engaged in activism and working as a steward to the land and are you wanting to create a difference?

Jackals do not have a glorified reputation. As scavengers, they are lumped into the category of rodents and pests. Is their ability to live off what others waste a negative thing or is it resourceful? Could they be considered masters of recycling? In every individual, whether that be human, plant or animal; there are dual attributes. For some people, to be referred to as a jackal is a bad thing and for others; it is a compliment.

If jackal comes through to you – whether in person, dream or meditation – pay attention. Maybe it is your inner duality that you must take to Anubis and weigh upon the scales? While many people new to the Craft shy away from the gods/goddesses which are considered '*dark, vengeful or death deities,*' I do not.

My goal is to live the best life I possibly can and to be of service to the goddess and all her children, plants, animals, and more. So, oftentimes I will seek out these darker deities to inquire as to what I can do more of, should be aware of and what would my ancestors in the Underworld like to see me do with this time I have on the planet?

To really activate connection with Jackal we are going to reach out to Anubis and see how we are measuring up, ask jackal how we can exert more agility and cunning wit to advance in a more productive way, or if we need to sit in the dark unknown a bit more...

BONUS – MEDITATION CONNECTION WITH ANUBIS AND JACKAL

For this connection, you may want to have a statue or image of Anubis and one candle.

Create a space where you will be uninterrupted and maybe even have another person lead you through this meditation, then offer it to them in return.

> Place your image or statue on a small table, the floor in front of you or on your altar.
> Begin with resting your eyes and focus on your breath.
> Inhaling to the count of four and exhaling to the count of four.
> Reminding your body that, as you move through this practice of focused breath work, you are releasing and letting go of all tension within the physical body.
> When your physical body is relaxed and your mind's eye open, you are ready to begin.
> See yourself in the desert. It is dusk and the Sun is fading, darkness is beginning to creep upon the sand that you sit upon. Before you are two small rugs and in the center a candle sits cradled by the red sand.
> Give yourself permission to sit upon one of the rugs and open your eyes long enough to light your candle and simply say: "Anubis I call to you. Anubis I honor you. Anubis I welcome you."
> Closing your eyes again and resting your mind, simply breathe until you feel a presence approaching.
> Before you walks a large man with the head of a jackal, or you may simply see a jackal.
> Watch as Anubis sits upon the other rug and faces you.
> In jackal or man/both form, offer Anubis gratitude for taking time to sit with you.
> See as he brings out his scale and without saying much he simply extends his right hand out and moves the scale closer to you. He doesn't say anything, he simply waits and watches with his great almond shaped eyes. What have you come to weigh? Place an item upon one scale that represents the works and deeds of your life so far. With his left hand

Anubis pulls a feather from his waistband and places it on the other scale. How does your life measure up so far?

Sit with Anubis and his scales for a moment or two.

What can you do more of in your life to make your ancestors proud and ensure a good life?

A good life, defined by your actions and interactions with others on this planet that we all share?

What are some things that have weighed you down and can those things be remedied?

Anubis puts down his scales and simply sits with you.

No words are spoken just energy shared between you.

When he is ready, he turns into full jackal and runs off into the distance.

The rug and scales dissipate into the sand. You look to the direction he ran and expect him to be long gone but instead, as jackal, he turns back to give you one last glance. A look of encouragement?

Maybe a glance to remind you that someone is always watching your deeds, whether it is the living or those in the Underworld.

JOURNAL PROMPT

Spend some time writing down your meditation experience. What did you weigh upon the scales? How do your works, deeds and actions so far in your life measure up? Would they make your ancestors proud? Is there more that you should be doing and can be doing?

STRATEGIZE

Make a list of all the things you are capable of doing more of. Then make a list of all the things you have done that can be mended and write down how you will mend those. You'll be surprised by the power of an apology and the magic that follows when you have righted a few wrongs.

Step into jackal mindset and scavenge up those parts of you that you maybe gave up on, or those mishaps that you thought could not be mended – exercise a new perspective and use that cunning wit to create change.

"Faith, like a jackal, feeds among the tombs, and even from these dead doubts she gathers her most vital hope."
Herman Melville

SEEING THE PEACOCKS IN YOUR LIFE

Peacock is a term to describe a male peacock bird. Females are called peahens. Their young are called peachicks. Males are not born with their extravagant feathers, in fact these feathers don't show up until the peachick is almost three years old. Peacocks are quite large and they can fly – just not very far.

In my brief journey into the world of law enforcement, while living at the Police Officer Standards and Training Facility for a six week period, each day began early! We were to be dressed in full uniform and ready for class by 7am. On alternate days, we were to be in gym attire and ready for two hours of physical and tactical defense training. One class really stuck with me and that was when we talked about 'peacocking' which by definition means "to display oneself ostentatiously."

Law enforcement officers have an incredibly difficult job and a very small number of them make this job even more difficult when they begin to peacock. In our training, the guest sergeant for the day gave a great demonstration of an officer peacocking. He stood extra tall, chest puffed out, legs a bit wider with a smug look of confidence on his face. We have all seen people peacock. Strutting their stuff as if to appear larger and more dominant. We were not being taught to peacock, we were actually being taught to NOT peacock. What happens when an officer peacocks is that they physically and energetically create a block where communication is very likely and respect is being demanded with use of a physical threat or show of power.

In life, we have all had experiences with peacocks. If you have ever seen a male peacock strut his stuff, it is quite the show. Peacocks fan out their exotic feathers to attract a mate. They are quite literally putting on a show. While, in the animal kingdom this is not an act of vanity or ego; it is the male's way of trying to impress the females, in the human kingdom, when someone struts – it is very much ego!

THE WHEEL OF THE YEAR

To better understand peacocks and ego, one needs to be aware of ego. By definition, ego is: "A person's sense of self-esteem or self-importance." In today's world of chaos and social media as the main outlet for seeking validation, more and more people are strutting – only, they have a screen to separate them. Social media has given us advances and disadvantages but what we are seeing is a rise in narcissism. People are able to create a whole new identity and with more likes, followers and subscribers; the validation and attention is just what a narcissist craves. Narcissism is defined as: "Excessive interest in or admiration of oneself and one's physical appearance."

The use of animals as mirrors is used so often in the way we talk, the way we refer to others and ourselves and psychologists have known for decades that we, as humans, are not so different from our animal relatives. Comparisons made between humans and animals helps us, as humans, understand certain characteristics that we are portraying.

There are many articles written by psychologists that are looking to the rise in narcissism as a rise in both peacock and ostrich characteristics. Some are overt and others covert. When working with others, it is important to have a basic understanding of the individual in general. What makes someone tick?

In this world of labels and boxes, that only create division, how can one move through the Wheel of the Year and still maintain an open heart and open mind?

What I found is that when you start seeing others as animals that softens your reactions. For example, I would never go up to a peacock on a farm and demand that it stop showing off. It's not showing off for me. Why care? Now, in the people world, when we see someone peacock, we tend to roll our eyes and disengage with some judgment thrown.

Whether someone is an ostrich and they are a closet narcissist with their head in the sand or a full-on peacock who struts about demanding that others bow down and pay homage to their grandiose larger than life display, our ability as individuals to react is the only thing we can control.

It is my belief that when a peacock person is strutting, rather than sit in awe at their ego on display, my gut response is to call them out on their insecurities, which is what they are really hiding behind those pretty feathers. It's important to honor the individuals but also to know when to engage and when to disengage.

In all the years of doing primary spirit animal readings, I have only had one peacock come through. By definition, this person was, and still is, a horrific narcissist.

When peacock people show up in your life, it's a challenge to not step into predator mode and visualize tearing them apart. Compassion is difficult with a narcissist and, really, it's just a waste of one's time. We can however look to them as a mirror of what 'not' to be.

The only reason I am including peacock in this section is to acknowledge that, yes, we have all at one time or another strutted our stuff and put on quite the display which, when we look back on – it is probably with an incredible amount of embarrassment. So, practice some compassion for yourself.

The other reason I have included peacock is to spotlight that, as individuals, we are fully capable and responsible for our interactions and reactions with others. Just like in law enforcement, when someone is peacocking, they are not approaching others with sincerity – they are displaying power. One can easily step into predator mode or prey mode. The key is; if you do choose to engage, then you own 100% of the consequences of that engagement.

TIPS FOR AVOIDING BEING ENTRANCED AND TAKEN ADVANTAGE OF BY PEACOCKS IN YOUR LIFE

- Use your legs and walk away. The best thing you can do with a narcissist and peacock person is to not give them the attention they are seeking. Walk away. Disengage.
- Don't waste your bite on someone who will take it as flattery. In other words; don't respond! Again, do NOT engage. Peacock birds are very territorial and are often used as 'guard dogs' on farms or estates. When you go after a peacock, whether animal or human, you are wasting precious energy

because you are now feeding them and giving their ego that precious desired attention and spotlight.
- You can honor an individual without being their best friend. As an animal-lover, I cherish animals; they are all unique and amazing. But just because I love animals and I am an animal activist does not mean I want to cuddle up next to all of them. I can see a peacock and admire its tenacity to put on quite the performance for the goal of enticing the opposite sex. I can see people who do the very same. But that's "not my circus, and not my monkey," so to speak. In other words; you don't have to like everybody. But you also don't have to be a jerk to everybody.
- See them for what they are; 'showing'. It is very rare in today's world to meet someone who is authentic and unafraid to be themselves in all situations. Part of me wants to be extra compassionate to peacock people because deep down they are usually hiding some heavy hurts and insecurities. But at the same time, I have been badly burned by peacock people, so giving them any of my precious time and energy is a self-defense mechanism that I acknowledge I have created. It's important to remember that no one really knows what is going on with another person as in our engagements in the world we really are only seeing what the other person wants us to see.
- Don't take it personally. This is difficult. History has shown that narcissists enjoy hurting others because they only care about themselves. In the peacock world, these birds are very social birds and very protective of their own. Some of us can relate to those attributes.

If peacock shows up as your mirror in life it is a good time to take inventory. Do some mirror work, shadow work and ask yourself what you are hiding behind those feathers?

Can you step into a space of humility and see that you do not need to strut around and demand the attention of others? Maybe you need to do some healing or humanitarian work to pull yourself out of the peacock strut.

JOURNAL PROMPT

Write down the times in your life when you have peacocked.

Then write down your reasons, why you felt the need and maybe reflect on other ways you could have handled the situation rather than peacocking.

LEARNING FROM THE SQUIRRELS

Squirrels are highly intelligent rodents in the family Sciuridae, which also includes ground squirrels, marmots, groundhogs, flying squirrels, chipmunks and prairie dogs.

Squirrels are deeply devoted to their survival. They spend their days in a constant state of gathering, building and caring for their families.

People who vibrate with squirrel energy are also deeply devoted to their personal and family survival. They spend all day in deep devotion to making sure everyone and everything in their house is in order.

Squirrels are excellent at remembering a kind face, especially one that comes with an offering of food. They are also brilliant communicators – from physically waving with their bushy tails to chirping and even barking.

Physically, these adorable bushy tailed creatures are in excellent health. With their keen eyesight, agility and quickness, squirrels know how to get around just about any situation. Apply that to a human and you find someone who is very active, quick to respond and very good at adapting to just about any situation.

Think of people in your life, do any of them have full closets for emergency preparedness? These preppers are stocked up and ready for the apocalypse! Do they work out often, maintaining their physical health and are they focused on home and family? Most likely, these people have some squirrel in them.

I can think of a few squirrel people in my life. They are masters of going and going and going, and then going some more. They have high energy and it is energy that does not go to waste. When I think of a squirrel person, I think of a person who has all their nuts in a row. They are prepared for everything!

We can learn to be more squirrel-like and it's really not that overwhelming. Squirrels mirror to us a balance of being prepared and the importance of having fun! If you think ahead about if you are prepared, then you don't need to scamper last minute. You have more free time and you can kick back and relax a bit. If squirrel shows up in meditation, in person or in dreamwork then you can safely say it's a good omen of encouragement to be prepared – stock up and get ready for winter, so to speak.

Once you have done the work and set the foundation, then spend actual playtime – quality time – with your family.

SQUIRRELS IN MYTHS AND LEGENDS

To the Celts, squirrels were messengers. They were also a source of food, so they were considered valuable. The Goddess Medb was depicted as warrior, resourceful, cunning, physically and mentally strong. She was said to have a squirrel that rode upon her shoulder and would (like Odin's ravens) go off and retrieve information and relay it back to her.

With the Norse legends, you have the giant warrior squirrel Ratatoskr, who is a symbol of rain and snow. It is told that he runs up and down the world tree, Yggdrasil, spreading false truths and enticing others into reacting.

In Hindu mythology, squirrels are sacred. It was squirrels who helped the Hindu God Rama cross the ocean between India and what we now know as Sri Lanka to bring back his kidnapped wife from the ten-headed demon Ravana. It is said that Rama was so grateful that he blessed the squirrels by touching their backs and that is why there are some species with stripes down their back.

Squirrels are even mentioned in Christianity, as a metaphor for hard work and being prepared.

HOW TO ACTIVATE YOUR INNER SQUIRREL

- Stop procrastinating! Don't wait to do something tomorrow that you can do today.
- Stock up! It doesn't hurt anyone to have a minimum of three months' supply of food, household supplies, plenty of

blankets and don't forget to stock up on your animals' food as well.
- Stock up also means set aside some money each paycheck. Build a healthy storehouse of funds.
- If you grow a garden – preserve it. The act of bottling, preserving and storing away your homegrown food and using it during the winter is also a perfect way to honor one's ancestors. You spend so much time working in the garden – don't let any of it go to waste.
- Be more active! Challenge your body. Participate in a workout group or boot camp. When we are physically active, it raises healthy endorphins. Healthy people are happy people!
- Work hard so you can play hard. Put in a full day's work! Get as much done as you can so you don't have to worry and stress later on. Then spend your evenings and weekends playing!

GREAT BUFFALO

These great and magnificent beasts were almost eradicated in the 1900's. If you want to see buffalo/bison in North America now then you need to travel to Yellowstone, where roughly 5,000 roam free. There is an estimated 500,000 across North America but these are typically interbred with cattle and privately-owned domestic livestock, raised in captivity as food.

When you think of the element of earth and attaching an animal that is of solid foundation, the buffalo is often called upon. These beasts are strong; they hold their heads up high and are a symbol of great power. Buffalo are herd animals and as such are family-oriented.

What if we opened our arms once more to the lessons animals have to teach us? Could we shift things on this planet? What if we centered our focus on family once again – the entire human species as one large family? What if we didn't focus on color, gender and politics? What if we cared for our elders, listened to their wisdom and ensured the survival of the young by changing how we live and the example we give them to follow? Like it or not, the little ones lead the way and they watch every little thing we do.

THE WHEEL OF THE YEAR

In witchcraft, when the north is called upon, typically the ancestors and bones of the ancestors are honored. When you think of the slaughtering of bison/buffalo in the late nineteenth century, there was unimaginable slaughter. These beasts were hunted down. I can't help but think of the scene in the movie *Dances with Wolves*, where Kevin Costner and the Native American tribe he has found home with come upon the herd of bison that have been mutilated by the thousands for their hide and horns; the meat was left to rot.

To the Native American tribes, bison/buffalo are honored and revered. These animals provided life to the tribe with their meat and their hides. They were seen as mothers who provided warmth and food. Massive symbols of balance and the mirror of what happens when we, as humans, turn into predators and take without consideration of the big picture.

Isn't it time that we honor the old ways by remembering that we do not own this land or the beasts that walk upon it anymore than we would want to be owned? We can stand together, hand in hand and be a force of inspiration and offer humility and gratitude. We can mindfully teach by example how to honor and hold sacred the plants, animals and each other. We can walk upon this earth with tenderness as if each step was a prayer of deep devotion. Just like in the legend of *White Buffalo Woman* who said: "Behold, me. For in a sacred manner I am walking."

Thich Nhat Hanh has said that we must "walk as if you are kissing the earth with your feet."

AKTA LAKOTA MUSEUM – LEGEND OF WHITE BUFFALO

One summer a long time ago, the seven sacred council fires of the Lakota Sioux came together and camped. The Sun was strong, and the people were starving, for there was no game. Two young men went out to hunt.

Along the way, the two men met a beautiful young woman dressed in white; she floated as she walked. One man had bad desires for the woman and tried to touch her. But, as he did this, the man was consumed by a huge cloud and turned into a pile of bones. The woman spoke to the second young man and told him, "Return to your people, and tell them I am coming."

This holy – wakan – woman brought a wrapped bundle to the people. She unwrapped the bundle, giving the people a sacred pipe and teaching them how to use it for prayer. "With this holy pipe, you will walk like a living prayer," she said.

The woman told the Lakota about the value of the buffalo, the women and the children. "You are from Mother Earth," she told the women. "What you are doing is as great as the warriors do."

Before she left, she told the people she would return. As she walked away, she rolled over four times. Then, she turned into a white female buffalo calf; hence the name White Buffalo Woman or White Buffalo Calf Woman.

It is said, after this important day, the Lakota honored their pipe, and buffalo were plentiful (from John Lame Deer's telling in 1967). Many believe the birth of the white buffalo calf 'Miracle' in the United States on August 20th 1994 symbolizes the coming together of humanity into a oneness of heart, mind and spirit.

> *"A white buffalo is the most sacred living thing you could ever encounter."*
> *John Lame Deer*

- For additional information on White Buffalo Woman, please read the book *Buffalo Woman Comes Singing* by Brooke Medicine Eagle.

MEDITATION CONNECTION WITH WHITE BUFFALO WOMAN

Please do this meditation outside, if possible.

> To make it a ceremony, create a circle of stones and sit inside the circle.
>
> In your mind's eye, prepare to enter a meditative space by focusing on your breath.
>
> Taking a slow intention focused inhale to the count of four, and a slow release with exhale to the count of four (repeat four times).
>
> With your physical body relaxed and you sit supported with earth beneath you, in your mind's eye bring your focus to where you are. See as if your eyes are opened your current surroundings.

Feel the elements upon you and within you. Allow the Mama, this sacred earth, to hold you.

Allow yourself time to honor any emotions that surface and welcome them as healing agents.

Allow yourself time to just be still and silent.

After some time has passed invite White Buffalo Woman to come to you.

Open your arms and be willing to receive her message in whatever form she delivers it.

She may appear to you as a woman dressed in white or she may appear as a white buffalo.

You may hear her voice upon the winds or feel her brush against you. Allow her to connect with you.

You may feel inclined to ask her what you can do to show your devotion to her, to show your devotion to earth. Feel as she sits beside you, she may hold your hand in hers.

She may offer you direction and ask you what you are already doing to show devotion.

You may feel inspired to ask for forgiveness.

Feel as Buffalo Woman blesses you with wisdom and grace.

JOURNAL PROMPT

Sit within your sacred ceremonial circle and write down any counsel you may have received from Buffalo Woman. Write down inspiration of how you can live a more devotional life.

> *"Buffalo Woman is calling. Will you answer her?*
> *She's calling light: she's calling peace.*
> *She's calling spirit: she's calling you.*
> *Buffalo Woman is calling. Will you answer her?"*
>
> *Brooke Medicine Eagle*

https://greateryellowstone.org/bison?gclid=EAIaIQobChMIjdn ErM7P8gIVOgytBh16IAeEEAAYASAAEgJBxvD_BwE

MOTHERLY MEDICINE OF OTTER

If you have ever seen an otter lounging on its back, cuddled up with its pups, enjoying the waves, then you know that otters are pure enjoyment.

It's easy to see the adorable pups and think that these animals are soft, cuddly and friendly. But no, they really are not!

Remember that ALL animals have both a predator and prey aspect. These are wild animals and they will, just like people, go to extreme lengths and scary tactics to protect their own.

ATTRIBUTES OF OTTER

Soft, cuddly, cute, muscular, predator, agile, resilient, powerful, long, slender, extremely intelligent, sustainable, strategic, territorial, maternal, aggressive and unpredictable.

SYMBOLS OF OTTER

Prosperity, good luck, loyalty, affectionate, caring, playful, transformation, mischievous, creative, survivalists, able to adapt, enjoying one's life.

WAYS TO ACTIVATE OTTER MEDICINE IN YOUR OWN LIFE

Gift yourself time to play. Spend time with your family and be creative.

Otter medicine is all about living in the moment. If you have a creative urge – activate it, don't put it off. If you are overwhelmed, kick up your feet and float in the magic of being present.

Kiss, cuddle and hug your loved one's often. There is a deep and profound magick that occurs when one steps into the realm of being present, conscious and mindful – you begin to see the signs and symbols in just about everything.

Just the other day, I was finishing up a four hour workshop on witchcraft. After the event, one of the attendees came to me and asked what the symbolism meant of the tiny winged beetle that was on her hand and would not leave.

My response was to let the guest know that she was already seeing the magick because she took the time to believe that there was something more than just a coincidence of a bug on her hand.

Step into the present moment! Laugh when something is funny and cry when you are floating on the waves of sorrow.

Just be! That is the secret to magick – being present.

"LET GO AND JUST BE" ACTIVATION MEDITATION CONNECTION WITH OTTER

In your mind's eye, move into a meditative space.

Simply and easily, bring your focus and awareness on your breath.

Taking a nice slow inhale and a nice and slow exhale.

Inhale to the count of four and exhale to the count of four.

Repeat for as many repetitions as you need until you feel your physical body relax.

In this state of mind, where the physical body has released all tension and the mind is clear and open, see and feel yourself in the middle of a large body of water. Water that holds you and lifts you up. Water that is clear and the waves are calm. Feel as you lie on your back simply float upon the gentle rocking movement of the water. Just rock side to side, bobbing up and down. Held by water, supported by and one with water. Activate your senses and feel the water, smell the water and breathe it in. Activate your inner otter and float – really float!

You will notice that the water is not too cold nor is it too warm, for you fur protects you.

The more held by water you are, the more waterproof your fur becomes; acting as if it is a life jacket, keeping you afloat. Just breathe! Just be!

JOURNAL PROMPT

Write down how it felt to just let go and float upon the waters.

ELEPHANT MEDICINE AND MAGICK

All hail the largest of all beasts upon the land! There are currently three species of elephant – the African bush, African forest and Asian elephant. They are the descendants of what are the now extinct mastodons.

Their extinct cousins are mammoths and straight-tusked elephants. Elephants are known for their superb memory; they can remember where watering holes are, even if they only visit them once in a decade. Out of all the land mammals, elephants have the largest brains.

These great masters can live to be 70 years old. They are matriarchal and the mother lineage is what determines the fate of the herd. She is the teacher – the transmitter.

Similar to box turtles, elephants can hear through the vibrations in the ground. In other words – through their feet.

They are very socially devoted to family and they are natural empaths – highly emotional beings. They can suffer from trauma just like we humans do. They remember those who hurt them. They experience PTSD (post-traumatic stress disorder) and they rely upon the elders in the herd to teach them, protect them and ensure their survival. When an elder or another one of the herd dies; the entire family pays their respects, mourning the loss for days.

ELEPHANT ATTRIBUTES

Some believe that the elephant is a symbol of good luck, prosperity, abundance, fertility, protection, wisdom and ancestral wisdom.

Similar to buffalo, these majestic creatures are connected to the element of earth and the direction of north.

LORD GANESH THE ELEPHANT GOD

"Om Gam Ganapataye Namaha"

In translation:

"Let's wake up root chakra energy of transformation so we can move through obstacles with ease."

All hail Lord Ganesh – he who removes the obstacles. The Hindu Elephant God Ganesh is called upon to clear anything that stands in the way of one's life and prevents them from moving forward.

While on a pilgrimage to Oregon to visit a sister goddess temple, my sister priestesses and I took a Sunday morning to soak in one of the natural hot springs. Whilst soaking, it didn't take long to recognize the God Ganesh as he sat, overseeing the pool from beneath his shrine, adorned with flowers, candles and offerings left by those who had paid homage.

Ganesh, Ganesha or Ganapati is an elephant. His name means 'Lord of the Ganas' or 'Lord of the People.' He is depicted as a rather pot-bellied, upright sitting elephant with four arms. He rides upon a rat and is therefore always depicted as having a small rat as his companion. In myth, Ganesha is accepted as the son of both Shiva and Parvati. He is also known as the God of New Beginnings.

RITUAL EXPERIENCE AND OFFERING TO GANESHA

Take some time and ponder the things in your life that you would describe as obstacles. Take inventory and actually write them down.

Create an itemized list or write them down on individual papers. Create a time in your schedule (preferably a Tuesday, as that is Ganesha's sacred day) that will be free from interruptions and remove all distractions.

You will need your list, a candle and a cauldron or fireproof bowl. If you have a statue or image of Ganesha then that is welcome too; but not necessary as your intent to call upon Ganesha can easily be done by simply stating his name.

In your quiet uninterrupted space, create your container in your own way, honoring your own tradition. Call to Ganesha – invite his presence to sit with you in the center. Light the candle.

> "Hail to Ganesha, Lord of New Beginnings.
> He who removes all obstacles.
> Hail Ganesha!
> I sing to you. I honor you.
> I bow to you.
> Ganesha, Ganesha, Ganesha."

Here in this space, begin to read out loud the obstacles you have written down. Take time to intentionally say them out loud and, after each one, recite: "I release you to Ganesha."

If you wrote them down on individual papers, slowly begin to light each one on fire after reciting the prayer and place them in the bowl to continue burning. Keep going until each obstacle is burned and removed.

Sit with Ganesha and remember what you saw as obstacles and asked to be removed – but you must also do the work – you must follow through! Ganesha will offer you strength and support but you must be willing to do the work yourself.

JOURNAL PROMPT

Write down how you felt going into the ritual and how you felt afterwards.

> "Like the rain would bless the earth,
> may Lord Ganesha bless you with happiness."
>
> *Ganapati Bappa Morya*

MYSTICAL UNICORN

Magical, mystical and legendary horses with a single horn atop their head, unicorns have always been mysterious, yet popular.

As a child, who didn't dream of owning a unicorn? I had a Huffy banana seat bicycle that I rode everywhere and in my imaginative play; she was the most enchanting unicorn.

Unicorns have been and still remain symbols of purity and innocence – a magick so raw and primal that one must seek to just catch a glimpse of it.

In the 1985 movie *Legend*, starring Tom Cruise, the unicorn represents the light of the world. In the story, the horn of the unicorn is so powerful that the Lord of Darkness is consumed with lust for it and targets the unicorn, knowing that to possess the horn of the unicorn is to rule the world and control the light.

In the *Harry Potter* stories, Professor Quirrell (who is a parasitic host of Lord Voldemort) must obtain unicorn blood in order to create the potion that would help a disembodied soul return to power.

Folklore from China, Japan, Greece and Scotland all has myths and legends about unicorns. Scotland loves the unicorn so much that it is their national animal. When my lover and I went on a pilgrimage to Scotland to uncover and connect with my ancestral bloodline, unicorns were depicted on tall buildings, churches and just about every shop had something with a unicorn on it.

To the Celts, unicorns possessed magical healing powers. They are courageous, strong, powerful, noble and pure. The horn of the unicorn contains healing properties. The Middle Ages were filled with legends, stories and sightings of these mystical beasts. They mirrored a wild freedom, intelligence and pure confidence – much like the Scottish people.

The very first depiction of a unicorn dates all the way back to 15,000 BCE in the Lascaux caves of modern-day France. In this cave system, there are over 2,000 animals represented, such as bear (which we saw and discussed earlier).

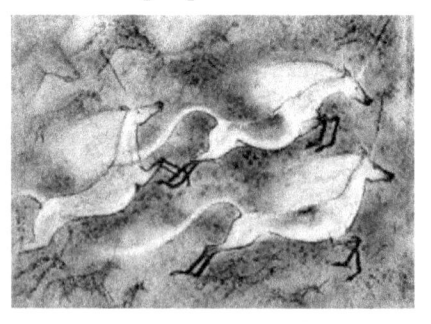

UNICORNS IN THE WORLD AROUND US

You have heard of alpha being used to describe people in the work place, despite 'alpha' being an outdated and misinformed modality.

Now you hear of unicorn people in the office. These are "special employees, respectful, hardworking and willing to wear many hats. They possess diverse skills, creative chops and are experts at data analytics."

Even in the world of dating and relationships, *unicorn* is a term that describes an individual who is willing to join an already existing relationship. One who becomes romantically involved with both members – a third.

> "Just because you haven't seen a unicorn doesn't mean they don't exist. Horses with horns on their foreheads who can only be approached by virgins are perfectly logical, their existence has not been confirmed yet."
> The Salesman in the 2017 film Unicorn Store

CREATIVITY AND UNICORNS

For me, unicorn medicine and magick takes me right back to my inner child; that time when I was seven and lived in my own world of make believe – that place where I didn't need to give an explanation or ask for permission, for I was the ruler of my world of play.

As adults, we do not play enough. We are busy! We have checklists of things that we have to get done each day in order for that day to be deemed productive – to the standards of society. Very rarely do we play. When was the last time you played dress up? Remember the *Friends* episode where the girls went to the bridal shop and all tried on wedding dresses? Now put unicorn heads on their bodies and you'll see the essence of unicorn coming through.

Any time we stop and shift focus to play and run wild, we are awakening the inner child and allowing the unicorn within us to emerge.

Think back on something you loved to do as a child. Write it down and then re-enact it! Put on something sparkly with tassels and really play! It's the little things that bring us joy. What if you put on a unicorn headband, sparkly wristbands and pranced around your own kitchen? This is a good start but there are always plenty of times to dress up and be a unicorn that would have made that little inner seven year old proud.

Be creative! Play! Dance, paint, laugh and be the unicorn. Be mysterious and unpredictable. Be bold, be true – be you!!!

ALWAYS BE YOURSELF.

UNLESS YOU CAN BE A UNICORN. THEN ALWAYS BE A UNICORN.

Unicorns are rare and I believe, as humans, our inner unicorns are also rare because we have been broken by society for so long that we have forgotten to be happy, to be present and to be … Just be.

This is a fun activity to do with others. After all, I think it's safe to say there is a little unicorn in each of us that just wants to get dressed up and have some fun. Maybe extend your invite to play?

PROTECTION OF DRAGONS

By definition, a dragon is: "A mythical monster like a giant reptile. In European tradition, the dragon is typically fire-breathing and tends to symbolize chaos or evil. In Asia, dragons represent fertility and are associated with the water and the heavens."

Just about every kid I have ever come into contact with has had a dragon stage. My daughter for a long time had an imaginary friend dragon named Herman.

Dragons, like unicorns, are often embraced as purely mythical or imaginative. Who hasn't grown up watching dragons on the big screen? Remember *Pete's Dragon*, the Disney film? Or, how about *DragonHeart*? Nobody can forget Smaug, the last great dragon to exist in Middle-Earth, from the *Hobbit* movies. How about when Daenerys Targaryen became mother to the three dragons in the *Game of Thrones* series? We can't forget Raya and her journey to find the last dragon. Even the new Marvel movie *Shang Chi* is rich with dragon lore and magic.

My favorite dragon series is the *How to Train Your Dragon* films. These are so well done and they really shift one's perspective from looking at dragons as monsters to seeing them as family.

For me, Falkor from the book and movie *The Neverending Story* is one of my most favorite dragons. In one passage in the book, Bastian describes his experience riding upon Falkor the Luck Dragon for the first time as follows: "This gentle rising and falling as the dragon adjusted his movements to the air currents was like a song, now soft and sweet, now triumphant with power. Especially when Falkor was looping the loop, when his mane, his fangs, and the long fringes on his limbs flashed through the air like white flames, it seemed to Bastian that the winds were singing in chorus."

Dragons will always have a special place in just about everyone's lives at one time or another. Just two days ago, I hosted a four hour event to introduce witchcraft to a nearby coven that was just getting started. One gentleman there stepped up to the altar to announce himself a witch of _____ (his fill in the blank was *dragons*).

In the Chinese zodiac, dragon represents power, luck, royalty, longevity, the ability to rebirth and hold magical powers. Dragons are mysterious, elusive, rare, protective, auspicious, strong and potent. They are keepers of the gateways to bodies of water.

When I do a house blessing and end with a shield of protection, it is usually a dragon that is called upon as sacred guardian and *watcher who sits on the roof.*

With there being hundreds of different branches or traditions, it really is no surprise that some practitioners honor the craft of sacred devotion to dragons.

Dragon magick and Draconian Wicca both center their solitary or coven work on dragons, rather than a deity.

Dragons have been called on as guardians, mirrors and teachers for centuries.

DRAGON ATTRIBUTES

Strength, resilience, power, ferocity, dominance, authority, bold, brave, noble, sometimes arrogant, ambitious and not afraid to conquer.

THE MINI DRAGONS IN OUR LANDSCAPES

Lizards are distant relatives to massive dragons. They are scaled, cold-blooded reptiles. Just like dragons, they rely on heat to sustain them. They are agile, capable of adapting to changes in their environment; they are quick and highly intelligent.

Next time you see a lizard sunbathing, and maybe doing little push-ups, just pause and think, "What if this tiny creature has dragon blood flowing within its veins," then offer it a song or chant of devotion: "Oh Great Lizard, I sing to you, I honor you, I bow to you."

Whether or not they are actually the descendants of great dragons and whether or not dragons really exist, when we offer an animal elevation we are reminding ourselves that we do not have dominion over the land and the animals.

We see them as DIVINE. We sing to them as SENTIENT BEINGS. We honor them as TEACHERS. We bow to them as MASTERS.

RING OF FIRE PROTECTION

To protect one's home, you can energetically call upon a dragon to sit on top of your roof and maintain protective presence.

I like to bump things up a bit, so I will have the dragon breathe a ring of fire that encompasses my home and boundaries of my property. This is done with visualization through meditation.

CALLING UPON DRAGON FOR ADDED PERSONAL PROTECTION

Let's face it; we are living in a very mean world. People are attacking each other left, right and centre over trivial things. Competition, contention and malice are spreading fast.

How can you protect yourself? Do you activate any energetic shields before you step out and enter the realm of the muggles?

What if you took three minutes and became thick skinned, like a dragon, before even leaving your car?

> Close your eyes and focus on your breath. Inhale to the count of four and exhale to the count of four.
>
> In your mind's eye, picture your skin starting to be covered with thick, impenetrable scales - the scales of a dragon. Feel your wings moving out of your spine and expanding down your arms.
>
> Stretch them, move them and know that energetically you can flee from any situation that harms your greatest good. Now focus on your eyes - your sight becoming more focused. Breathe into your tailbone and allow it to extend down and out, creating a long thickly scaled tail. Feel your teeth growing large and sharp, your breath hot as if each exhale is releasing fire. Here you are dragon.
>
> Protected - your scales thick. Any energy sent your way simply hits the scales and falls to the ground where it is absorbed and transformed by the Mama, Mother Goddess - Nature herself.
>
> When you are ready to take off your dragon armor, you simply close your eyes and give thanks to the scales, feeling them slough off as you move your body. Give thanks to your focused eyes and your hot breath of fire. Breathe in, pull in your tail. Allow dragon energy to dissipate as you bring your focus back to your human self once more.

DRAGON SCALES

As an animist, working with stones, crystals and gemstones is just like working with other people – it is unavoidable. My favorite stone (which I refer to as 'stone people') is Labradorite. To me, it looks like dragon scales. Because I am very family-oriented, children are a constant in my life. Nothing shifts a toddler's temper tantrum more than if you ask them if they want to hold a dragon scale.

Labradorite is a feldspar mineral. It is useful for the crown, brow and throat chakra. It is associated with the zodiac signs of Leo, Scorpio and Sagittarius. Its element, just like dragons; is water.

This stone is all about transformation and balance. It is powerful in allowing one to see through the illusions and find the truth. Labradorite stones, like dragons, are protection stones. They banish fear and strengthen confidence. Some refer to Labradorite as the 'stone of magic' or 'Keeper of the Northern Lights.' Hold a Labradorite up to the Sun and watch the spectrum of colors dance in bright hues of greens, blues and purples. Monica Vinader writes in her blog: "Legend has it that one of the greatest natural shows on earth, the Aurora Borealis, was trapped inside the rocks of Labrador and lay awaiting discovery amongst the Inuit and Beothuk people."

> "It simply isn't an adventure worth telling if there aren't any dragons."
>
> *J.R.R. Tolkien*

ROADRUNNER THE LUCK BRINGER

Roadrunners are long legged, speckled members of the cuckoo family. They are common in the southern United States and Central America.

If you're lucky, you may catch a glimpse of one running by. They are fast – reaching speeds of up to 20 mph. They are known as terrestrial birds which is a fancy word meaning that they stay on the ground. Roadrunners can fly but not far distances, they prefer to walk or run, similar to their other terrestrial bird relatives, such as emus, quails, pheasants, guinea fowl, turkeys and kiwis, to name a few.

Growing up, my only real exposure to roadrunners was from the Looney Tunes cartoons on TV on Saturday mornings. Now that I live out in the desert, I have seen a few, but it is a pretty rare sight.

For some Native American tribes, the roadrunner is a sign of good luck. As a mirror, roadrunners show us the capability of being quick! Moving fast towards something in a confident and motivated manner is all roadrunner medicine. They are also spiritual messengers. It's safe to say that if a roadrunner crosses your path, an unexpected message is on its way. These fast dinosaur-like birds also remind us to be quick to take action

– be alert and maintain excellent physical health so that you are prepared for whatever comes your way.

GENTLE CALM OF THE MANATEE

While on a family vacation to Georgia, we had the opportunity of having a beach day.

Ocean magick is so rare and exciting for us desert dwellers that we just ran into the ocean without really considering who or what we were swimming with.

It was rumored that just days before an alligator had been spotted on this very beach. So, while I was out with my two young boys, watching them splash about with their cousins, all my hunches raised when I saw two dark things swimming rather close to my children.

As calmly as I could, I went over to the children and told them to get out of the water, that there was something swimming with them. Well of course, you can probably hear their shrieks as they ran, not so calmly, out of the water.

The two figures swimming just inches away from my boys were in fact two manatees, otherwise known as the cows of the sea. Manatees are large aquatic mammals. These gentle giants are very docile and calm. Their existence is very much under attack from the world's number one predator: humans.

While they are mostly solitary, they spend their days napping and grazing in the shallow waters. They are known to have a good long-term memory and, much like dolphins, are quite excellent communicators.

Spiritually, manatees mirror to us the importance of slowing down, taking deep breaths and embracing calmness. They are the medicine mirrors of breath work. Their lungs are unique – they lie long and flat, lengthwise along the back. This gives them the ability to take in more oxygen with each breath. Manatees can exchange 90% of the air that is in their lungs in just one single breath. They inhale and exhale through their nostrils only and can stay underwater for up to twenty minutes on just one breath.

When I think of the medicine of the manatee, the Simon & Garfunkel song *Feelin' Groovy* comes to mind.

How can you benefit from manatee medicine? Are you ready to slow down and just breathe?

> "Slow down, you move too fast
> You got to make the morning last
> Just kicking down the cobblestones
> Looking for fun and feeling groovy
> Ba da-da da-da da-da, feeling groovy"

https://www.savethemanatee.org

ARMADILLO

Sometimes referred to as the 'turtle rabbit', the armadillo is like a tiny gladiator.

Armadillos are covered with bony plates otherwise known as armor. They rely upon their ears and nose more than their eyes to detect food or predators. They like water and are very good swimmers. They also enjoy digging.

If armadillo has made contact with you, it is time to ask yourself: "Why are you so guarded?" You may have to 'dig deep' to discover what it is you are armored against in life. Do you have a shield up? Are you hiding from your true self? Or are you not shielding yourself enough?

If armadillo has appeared to you, I suggest water for meditation. Get a bath going, light some candles and do some deep breathing.

Ask armadillo to help you understand what layers of armor you need to remove or how many layers of armor do you need to put on?

Remember that armadillo is your guide, so be open to receive its messages.

ALLIGATOR

Often referred to as 'gators', they are different to crocodiles. Alligators can be distinguished by their wide, rounded snout and black color.

Alligators are social creatures and live in congregations. They enjoy swimming and basking in the Sun. Alligators hunt in water and can swim very quickly after their prey. They are strictly carnivores. They can also hold their breath under water for four to fifteen minutes but can remain under water for up to two hours if needed.

If alligator has made contact with you, it is time to recognize that you have the ability to withstand whatever life throws at you. You also have the ability to speak your truth so don't be afraid to 'snap your jaws' at those who are or have been walking all over you. You have the right to speak up for you and sometimes a simple 'snap' will give a clear message.

Alligators have ancient magick and it may be best to do your meditation in water as well. Have a nice warm bath and ask alligator what its message for you is.

Are you supposed to lie low and observe or are you supposed to venture out knowing you are heavily protected by armor and sharp teeth to address the issue at hand? Whatever the message – remember to be open.

OCTOPUS

Out of all the creatures of the sea, the octopus is the most intriguing – at least for me, personally.

These fascinating, agile and incredibly intelligent beings have three hearts, nine brains and each arm consists of 40 million neurons! That is beyond belief but very true.

Octopuses are members of the family Cephalopoda, which consists of over 300 species. They grow quick and die young – typically living up to an age of between three to five years. They are considered by most biologists to be the most highly evolved invertebrate.

When working with or honoring one's inner octopus, acknowledging one's intelligence is just natural. Maybe you have been working incredibly hard on a project and are finally seeing the results? Maybe you used strategy and maneuvered yourself out of a tight situation and are now swimming free?

Octopus can also show up in your life to remind you of your potential. It may be time to swim into your own depths and embrace your mysterious self with all eight of your legs.

Let octopus mirror to you flexibility, mystery, adaptability and the art of being unpredictable.

To truly connect with the energy and medicine of octopus, let's journey through meditation:

Begin with your breath.

You may find this meditation helpful to do in a shallow swimming pool or bathtub.

Sitting in water can be very grounding.

With your focus on your breath, take a nice slow and conscious inhale, then exhale fully.

Allow your body to relax and exhale out and away any tension, bringing yourself into a physically safe and comfortable state of just being present with breath.

As you sit here, with your eyes closed, tap into your mind's eye – your source of imagination – and see yourself in clear blue waters.

There is sand beneath you and you are gently floating in the water.

Begin to slowly move your arms through the water with grace.

Imagine what it would be like to have eight arms, eight arms that all have their own brain!

What could you accomplish with eight arms? What could you touch, feel and experience?

Begin to think on all the things you could do and feel as those eight arms begin to connect to you. Watch and observe. Your arms may look like your arms or they may look like the arms of an octopus. See them for what they are and, just for a few deep breaths, connect with the possibilities and connect with the water. When you have experienced the medicine of octopus, slowly begin to bring your awareness back to your current physical surroundings. Begin to move your fingers and your toes, moving your arms. See your arms in their natural state. Knowing that you can connect with octopus at anytime, you close your eyes and envision it. But for now, return to this here and this now.

JOURNAL PROMPT

Write down all the things you could accomplish if you had eight arms. Would being able to accomplish these things in a quicker manner be helpful in your current situation or do you merely need to reprioritize them?

KRAKEN

While some believe the Kraken to be simply mythical, others firmly believe in its existence and honor it as a sacred animal messenger. The Kraken is said to be a giant creature that looks similar to a squid.

Most sightings were stories told by sailors returning home from voyage around the thirteenth century.

While the octopus is graceful, gentle and more of a problem solver, the Kraken is fierce, greedy and would supposedly swallow entire ships with all on board.

You may be wandering why I would even bring up the Kraken as having medicine and magick that one would want to embody?

Well the Kraken, like any 'shadow' side, is shocking, powerful and revealing. They serve as reminders and mirrors of the depths that we oftentimes try to keep hidden. Sometimes we exert so much energy burying things which we feel are better off forgotten, that we end up being entangled and later drown from the weight of them.

The Kraken, as teacher, offers us primal, raw and emotional release! Can you stay afloat in the rocky waves of life or will you be pulled under? For most animal guides, the Kraken is the mirror of subconscious fears and wounds that need to surface. They offer a reminder to first heal oneself before offering healing to others.

When embracing any animal as a mirror, it is important to ask questions. Why tentacles? What do they represent? If the Kraken was a fierce creature that would drag entire boats under the water consuming everything and then regurgitating the debris back onto the surface of the water to attract other prey, are you the boat full of people or are you the Kraken? If you are the Kraken, why go to all that trouble to conquer if you are just going to vomit it all back up? Was it all a show?

CHAPTER TEN

Desert Sage Witchcraft – Practicing Animism Solitary and/or within a Pack

As a triple ordained Wiccan high priestess, it has been my privilege, honor and service to represent the three lineages I am ordained within.

Dianic Wicca has gifted me a space to circle with women only and honor goddess only. This space is ideal for those women who are healing from patriarchy and/or abuse from men.

For me, anchoring in the Dianic tradition felt like secret magick, the kind of magick where you sneak off into the woods late at night to circle with your best girlfriends. It is a beautiful tradition and I love my Dianic space. For six years, I led a Dianic coven and that was an extreme learning curve and upheaval, filled with amazing rituals and much drama.

In the Alexandrian/Hermetic lineage. I have found balance, structure and very 'cut and dried' rituals that, although spelled out and almost scripted, gifted me a new outlook and perspective on larger circles and the dynamics necessary to bring large groups into a ritual mindset.

The eclectic Wicca lineage is much more open and diverse, dabbling into all sorts of lineages and compiling them into some form of structure that fit myself and the group I was circling with. I like eclectic, up to a point, but it has felt too open and there are not enough boundaries, which for me I prefer; some sort of structure and direction.

After 26 years actively engaged in my solitary witchcraft practice, one thing I have learned is that taking any tradition, whether it is of Wicca or witchcraft, is best if anchored into one's own landscape and lifestyle.

Although I am ordained within these three traditions and I do honor them very deeply, it has been very important for me to step in fully and birth my own tradition and offer yet one more branch or tradition to the large tree of Paganism.

When I travel and teach the differences between witchcraft, Wicca and Paganism, I take with me a painting I did of a large tree with long roots that go deep into the ground. This tree represents Paganism with its roots anchored into agricultural, Nature-based practices.

On this tree are many, many branches which represent the different Wiccan and witchcraft traditions that are practiced today. So, as a Wiccan, I honor deeply the Dianic, Alexandrian/Hermetic and eclectic traditions. As a witch, I honor the green, kitchen, hedge and animistic paths.

Desert sage witchcraft is technically a Wiccan tradition, as it does have a hierarchy or a structure and we do circle casting. This tradition is anchored in Celtic and Nordic Totemism, with Gardnerian and Alexandrian roots. My ancestry is Celtic, English and Nordic. So, when birthing this tradition, it was vital to honor my blood and the ancestors upon whose shoulders I stand.

The common focus of desert sage witchcraft is: "Totemism – a kinship or mystical relationship with a spirit-being, such as an animal or plant. The entity, or totem, is thought to interact with a given group or individual and to serve as their emblem."

Desert sage witches honor the wolf as mirror, example and prime totem. So instead of forming a coven (which is thirteen or less witches), or a grove (which is thirteen or more), in this tradition we form a wolf pack.

Desert sage witches look at ALL animals as examples, teachers, messengers, guides and mentors of how best to live their practice of being an animistic witch on a day to day 'eat, sleep and breathe' basis, whilst under the keen observation and teachings of a mama wolf and/or papa wolf.

While the ranking and essence of the wolf pack is the basis of our tradition, within the realm of desert sage witchcraft we honor that each individual may connect with and honor a different animal and/or insect, fish, etc. as their primary and self-dedicated totem.

It is up to the individual to implement their solitary animal mirror and collectively bring those authenticities into the den when we circle as a pack.

As desert sage witches, we honor each individual and as such do not implement belief systems or ways of living one's solitary practice. We honor that when individuals are in their own homes, practicing their own Craft, they are in complete and absolute control and do not answer to anyone other than their own selves.

This tradition stems from the magick, heat and necessity of the desert. It is anchored in the practice that magick comes from the ground up, from the source of the Mother's belly and a deep and profound connection to the animals, plants and seasons of one's own desert.

In this tradition one bows deeply to the Mama – she being the Earth herself as the source of knowing – the provider and the one who holds the wisdom and key to our survival.

Unlike other traditions, there is not a god or goddess that is honored. Instead each ceremony honors the attributes of an animal.

Our Wheel of the Year actually features all of the ceremonies found within this book. These are actual ceremonies that have been utilized here at our home base, the Utah Goddess Temple, where we as a wolf pack of about thirteen to thirty people circle often. This is our den, our safe space, our tangible physical Pagan sanctuary.

While we are a diverse group of individuals who all practice their own unique solitary Wiccan, witchcraft or Pagan traditions, making the shift from a grove to a wolf pack was not difficult and everyone that we circle with actually felt a more welcomed shift because of it.

In a wolf pack, there is a natural hierarchy. It is accepted, not resisted. While, for decades, it was readily accepted that there was an alpha male and alpha female, this modality is no longer used nor was it ever accurate.

An alpha is one who rules with force, dominion and aggression. Wolves are very family-oriented; everything a wolf does is for the better of the pack as a whole. The one who leads the pack did not earn its position by force or by fighting and winning against the former leader. The ones who lead the pack are the ones who birthed the pack – literally.

A wolf pack has a mama and a papa or Mother Wolf and Father Wolf. They quite literally birthed the pack into existence. They are the ones that nurture, grow and ensure the wellbeing of each individual in the pack.

In today's modern Pagan revival traditions, those new to the Craft are sadly often referred to as 'baby witches'. However, in desert sage witchcraft, we call them pups. A slight shift in language creates a slight shift in acceptance. I have found that the more people are open to animals, then allowing an individual to see within themselves an animal is easier.

So, referring to someone who is new to the Craft as a pup is more accepted than the over used label of 'baby witch'.

At the Utah Goddess Temple, where I serve my community as high priestess, I am not referred to as priestess (except by those who've circled with me before, in a very traditional Alexandrian grove). I am referred to as Mama Wolf or my official title of Lady Wolf, which was given to me by Zsuzsanna Budapest during my Dianic ordination, back in 2018.

As Mama Wolf, it is my devotion to ensure the wellbeing of all who circle here in our pack. One way we do this is to include everyone! In other traditions, I have found that exclusion is prevalent. While each tradition has its own agreements and ideals, beliefs and unique practices that set them apart from each other, what I didn't like was the act of excluding others. So, things needed to shift.

When wolf came to me as teacher, things shifted here regarding the work, direction and focus we were birthing at Utah's FIRST dedicated Pagan temple.

As a Nature-based Pagan practice, honoring our local landscape was something else that needed to happen as the desert sage witchcraft tradition was being birthed. It is often hard to celebrate the Celtic Wheel of the Year here in the desert when we do not ride the wet season of the UK.

We frequently had to adapt our ceremonies to make them fit with the current season happening here in our High Desert.

For example, Imbolc is typically a sabbat that welcomes the quickening of spring with snowdrops and daffodils. Here, where I live, we are usually still tucked under a thick blanket of white snow at this time. So, no flowers.

Imbolc is also centered on milk – the first milking of lambs. Not something we have here in the desert around the time Imbolc is celebrated which is February 1st.

So, instead of working with lambs, we honor Mother Bear who is starting to slowly awaken from her winter sleep.

Desert sage witchcraft utilizes the desert as the great metaphor of life. The energy of the desert is a source of spiritual guidance. The desert provides us with heat, LOTS OF HEAT! That heat, when felt physically, can be overwhelming, exhausting and painful.

But in all of this there are teaching moments that are anchored into a need to survive. Desert magick is all about harnessing survival techniques to amplify one's solitary practice with the hopes of helping others through service to see and understand that, no matter the heat, fear or challenges that surface when in the desert, the Great Source always provides a rescue and remedy.

Let's enter the desert!

> In your mind, picture yourself walking in the desert.
>
> Give yourself permission to see the dirt, connecting with this landscape, really seeing each tiny grain. What color is your dirt in this desert of your mind? Are you barefooted or do you have shoes on?
>
> Is the dirt hot? What time of day is it in this desert? Now see the sky. Is it clear?
>
> Are there clouds in your sky above? Now see around you, what plants, if any, are growing?
>
> Listen – do you hear any animals? Do you see any animals?
>
> In this, the desert of your mind, how is your physical body responding? Are you excited? Anxious? Hot? Thirsty?
>
> Simply honor each feeling that surfaces; knowing that desert magick is all instinctual.
>
> It is primal. It is raw and stems from a need to survive.
>
> Walk the desert, no destination in sight, no pathway already placed before you.

Right here, right now, is just you. Just you and the heat of the desert.

There has to be an uneasiness as you embark upon any new journey. There has to be discomfort, apprehension and a bit of fear to challenge you on this journey, otherwise how else will you grow? How else will you own your own survival? Nothing is going to be handed to you in this desert.

You must do the searching, you must seek the answers.

You must anchor into your truth, no matter what obstacles or environment you enter.

Just be.

JOURNAL PROMPT

What feelings surfaced in the heat of your desert?

Write them down and allow yourself a day to process and see them for what they are.

SPIRALING IS PART OF THE JOURNEY

Every Wiccan, witch or Pagan tradition, branch or practice, has its own symbols and sigils. In desert sage witchcraft the main symbol is the spiral.

In the desert journey, one will face many challenges and obstacles. These will be mirrors and opportunities for shadow work to surface, or rather – these are times to venture deep into one's *inner desert*. In this tradition, we walk a spiral. Not a circle!

For life is all one tiny spiral after another. Each spiral is a journey inward and a journey outward – there is no such thing as getting stuck. For, in a spiral one cannot get 'stuck'. One is constantly moving.

As we begin each spiral, we are the ones who determine the speed at which we travel and the length of our stay within each spiral.

Walking the desert spiral is a simple technique used to anchor into one's own landscape and honor the individual path. So, stand up! Wherever you are, walk a spiral....

As you journey into the spiral, think of those attachments that you have made, about who you are. Think of the roles, responsibilities and titles that you have allowed to become tethered to who you are and let them fall.

In the desert, it is hot so we disrobe energetically and spiritually. We have to strip away all of these so that we can enter the desert and find ourselves. We have to remove all the anchors that once defined us so that we can be in the center of the desert spiral and awaken to our truth.

As animists, we see the divine in all things. This includes oneself! So, in a standing position, let's activate the many spirals that are within us. Begin with your ankles and start a rotation, making sure to honor both directions and both ankles.

Send this rotation up your legs in whichever way you choose. Then move to your hips, moving them around and around, until your torso and center begins to spiral up to your chest, your arms, neck and head.

This is similar to belly dancing and warming up the body, only that our focus is activation of spiral energy from toe to head. Now we empower it with intention and we awaken our physical altar to prepare for our spiral journey.

SINGING A SONG OF WELCOME TO THE ANIMALS OF EACH DIRECTION

What makes desert sage witchcraft a Wiccan tradition is that the ceremonies are held within a cast circle.

While each element is called (such as east to south, south to west, west to north and north to east), instead of calling upon a god or goddess; an animal is invoked and greeted with each directional element.

WE BEGIN BY FACING THE EAST

What does east magick feel like to you? In most traditions the east honors the air. In desert sage witchcraft, the east also represents the air.

Think of standing in the hot desert and the east is the breath of a goddess, blowing in refreshing change, a cool breeze, or it brings an almost suffocating force of intense heat and power such that it becomes hard to breathe.

The Air is a force. In this tradition, we will not spend time focusing on the properties of air, rather we will focus on the animals that rely upon air – the winged ones. In this tradition we honor the animal teachers in our own actual landscape, we connect with the winged ones that live in our physical environment.

Please take some time and observe the birds or winged insects in your local area and focus on three different species. Journal about each one. What kind of birds or winged insects are you connecting with? What do they look like? What do they eat? How do they create their own space?

Your second assignment is to learn about their life phases. Each animal or insect, much like us humans, go through phases. What do those look like?

In this tradition, unlike others in the past, we connect with the 'fledgling' phase of winged ones. You may relate this to the 'maiden' or 'page' in other traditions.

With the energy of fledgling we are very much settled into the energy of the east – the place of new dawns, new days and new beginnings.

What does it mean to you to step into fledgling? What physical attributes does the fledging possess? Do you see the similarities?

By honoring and becoming acquainted with the winged ones in your natural environment you deepen your connection to your landscape and step into practical priestess work, which is all about connecting to your natural surroundings.

We are not pulling information from a pantheon outside and away from you. Rather, we are creating a pantheon within you, based on where you actually live. This is vital in desert sage witchcraft as the only way to connect with the elements, animals and plant allies in this tradition is to focus on the ones you actually see, hear, feel and experience on a day to day basis. So go outside and really connect.

If you find it difficult to see or connect with an actual winged one then do some research and try a trial and error approach. What time of day in the desert are the winged ones active? What are they eating and how can you attract them into your physical location?

Let us sing a song of welcome with our arms open as if they are wings, extending out, hopeful to hop up, lift off and take flight:

> "I sing to the east, I sing to the air, I sing to the winged ones,
> please join me here, please join me here, please join me here."

In the place of 'winged ones' place the name of an actual bird from your own landscape. For example, one of my local birds is the 'mourning dove'.

Because this tradition is all about connection and activation through movement and embodiment, each time we sing to the east – we honor how our arms are our wings – those extensions of our energy and ability to reach out, expand and open ourselves up to connecting with the winged ones of the east, those young ones who are brave, bold, unsure and forced to activate their survival instincts in order to take flight and soar.

TURNING TO THE SOUTH

Take inventory of your landscape. What reptiles live nearby? All too often, we humans rely upon others to be our source of heat, passion and fuel. We look outward instead of inward.

We rely on summer and the Sun to be our heat. We become depressed in winter because we are lacking warmth and sunlight. We become victims of our own doubts and insecurities. We fall prey to what society has taught us – that in the winter we are supposed to get seasonal depression. This is false.

While physically, our bodies may be lacking the nutrients to be in balance, we still have the control and we still have ways of creating heat. It may be helpful to research local lizards. When we take time to dive into lizard magick, it doesn't take long to connect them to dinosaurs.

These great giants left behind a legacy that still today humankind finds fascinating and much-unknown. These majestic reptiles left tracks in the sand that have become fossilized and preserved and we have embraced their legacy and developed a hunger to learn more.

Where in the east, we sang to the fledging birds; in the south we call to the hatchling lizards. The hatchling lizard is ready to create; to birth into existence and experience the passion of life. The reptile hatchling is quite the opposite of an altricial bird hatchling. Most hatchling reptiles are born with the same instincts as their parents and leave to live on their own immediately after exiting the egg.

This is all south energy! Harnessing that power, heat, passion, sexuality of calling in the energies of the fire – lizards rely upon the Sun for their very survival.

We too are animals and we need the Sun!

With hands held over your source of fire and physical creation, welcome the powers of the south, activate the lizard within and sing the next verse in our song of welcome:

"I sing to the south, I sing to the fire.
I sing to the .... (lizard of your choosing).
Please join me here. Please join me here. Please join me here."

FACING THE WATERS OF THE WEST

Why is the west associated with water? Where did this information come from? How many other religions, pantheons and cultures honor water – connected with the direction of west?

When I began birthing this tradition, I thought of the zodiac. Scorpions roam everywhere in my yard and they are attached to water. I also have seen salamanders and toads.

The west is where you find healing and motion. So, when deciding what water animal to select, make sure that you feel comfortable working with that particular animal and then research that animal extensively!!!

When you stand to sing a song of welcome to anything or anyone, it is important that you know which attributes you are inviting. It is also important in animism that you understand and honor the power of water. Not just the water you consume, but the waters of life. Your blood! How does it flow? What does it provide for you? When you greet the element of water how can you communicate the power of water with words?

MAKE A LIST

List descriptive water words (please fill an entire journal page) that you can begin to apply and connect with animals and your own inner flow of emotions.

Then write on the top of a new page: "Today I am ………" Then write one water descriptive word: "………." Then record your emotion: "………."

For example: "Today I am floating in my chosen insecurities."

When we attach water descriptions to our feelings, we honor them as fluid and can better allow them to surface and flow down and out instead of anchoring into them as truth. Emotion, like water, ebbs and flows, like the tides of the ocean. We give each wave of emotion sensations and energy.

When we combine water with our animals, we begin to feel the energy of fluid motion coursing through the ceremony as we sing to the west:

> "I sing to the west, I sing to the waters.
> I sing to the ………. (water animal of your choosing).
> Please join me here. Please join me here. Please join me here."

TURN TO THE NORTH

Here in the north, we call to the animals that honor and represent the earth. What land animals (or underground ground animals) do you have in your own landscape or backyard? What are your native animal messengers?

Here in my desert we have prairie dogs, skunks, antelopes and coyotes, to name but a few.

Take some time and get to know, to the best of your ability, at least three local land animals. What characteristics and attributes do they have that you admire? What similarities do you share with them? One of these animals will be your anchor to the element of the north by helping you connect with the land.

When we face the north, we call upon and activate the bones, history and magick of the ancestors.

HONORING THE TRACKS – HONORING THE ANCESTORS

All too often, I hear young witches think they are alone, walking a path that is completely new. While in some ways, in this lifetime, when we discover witchcraft it is new in actuality; our spirit is ancient. We have all lived many different lifetimes as many different beings and entities.

So, in actuality, we are not walking a new path – for we have done this before. There has always been someone or something that has walked before us, leaving tracks, breadcrumbs and insights for us to follow. Someone left us a legacy.

These land animals leave literal tracks in the sand. In this path, let us not step into ego and arrogance and think that we are reinventing the wheel – we are not walking an unknown path.

Even this tradition is not 'new', for it is anchored in ancient wisdoms those of animism and Totemism. Our implementation and interpretation may be new for us as individuals, but make no mistake; this is not new.

We have blueprints, stories, clues and tracks left in the sand for us to follow, but we are the ones that choose which legacy we follow and which legacy we leave behind.

Do you know your ancestry? Do you know where your ancestors came from?

The United States is a very young country and incredibly ignorant in many ways. We are actually living in a country that is currently embracing erasure of history because we "don't like it."

But, guess what? You cannot undo something that has already been done. We have to look back in order to know how to move forward and adapt to our current situation, for the past is the past and we are the ones that create the future.

SPEND TIME DISCOVERING YOUR DNA

Find out who your ancestors were. Talk to your relatives and ask questions. Listen to the stories.

In which ways can you carry on their legacy? In which ways are you carrying on their legacy?

MOST IMPORTANTLY, WHAT IS YOUR LEGACY?

You are currently creating tracks in the sand. Who will follow your tracks? Who will pass on your stories? Who will see what you have created and share it? Who will pick up your breadcrumbs and move forward to create their own legacy because you helped pave their way?

When you select an animal to sing a welcome song to when facing the north, maybe it is an animal that comes from your ancestry? Do you have a family crest or coat of arms? As one whose ancestry stems from Scotland, my family crest contains the stag. So, one animal I have sung to in the north is the just that: the stag.

When you have an animal, crouch down upon the ground, on all fours and sing:

> *"I sing the north, I sing to the earth.*
> *I sing to the .... (earth animal of your choosing).*
> *Please join me here. Please join me here. Please join me here."*

Another thing you can do if you are not able to find or locate animals that correspond with each elemental directional is go through meditation and seek out animal messengers.

For example, you can meditate and visualize being in the water and call upon a water animal to find you and connect with you.

Once you have an animal for each direction, you are ready to put it all together and cast your sacred vessel for ceremony, spell work and solitary or pack magick.

PUT IT ALL TOGETHER IN SONG AND DEVOTION:

Go outside to your earthing spot and face the east – it's time to sing! To put it all together. Be sure and attach your individual animals to each direction as you turn the wheel of directions within and without:

> *"I sing to the east, I sing to the air, I sing to the .... Please join me here.*
> *I sing to the south, I sing to the fire, I sing to the .... Please join me here.*

I sing to the west, I sing to the water, I sing to the .... Please join me here.
I sing to the north, I sing to the earth, I sing to the .... Please join me here.
I sing to above, I sing to below, I sing to the center now my ...... is whole."

The last blank is for you to fill in.

When we sing this song of welcome inside the goddess temple, we fill in the blank with *temple*. Be creative! Is it a circle that you are casting with song? Or an egg?

What best describes your sanctuary? Use that word to fill in the last blank.

LIVING THE DESERT SAGE PATH DAY TO DAY:

This is a path and tradition of mindfulness, being conscious and allowing animals to guide you through the Wheel of the Year... Each year!

A good start to your day would be to greet the Sun. For me, I go out each morning, extend my arms up and open, and then I call out a welcome to the Sun. What will be your welcome? How will you greet the Sun or will you sing a song of greeting to the fledgling birds?

Observe the times of day that you are most active. For me, it is definitely in the morning and evening. Midday is hard for me because it tends to get so hot!

Once you have found your 'power' time of day, research which animals embrace this time of day as well. Write down and use them as mirrors to help you embrace the similarities that you may share.

You may find it helpful to work with this time of day on manifesting a deeper connection to the particular animal(s) that you have embraced. They are teachers, so take the time to have an open heart and invest in the lessons they provide.

Winding down one's day is a good way to show appreciation and honor all the lessons, teachers and messages you may have received. Oftentimes we do not even realize they were there until we sit down to write them down. Take time to reflect in a manner of gratitude.

Moving through this consciously connected day to day intention of being aware of the animals, plants and seasons creates a very intimate and powerful relationship with the landscape and solitary practice one lives.

SCORCHING IN THE DESERT

Go into your meditative state and enter the desert – go midday, when the Sun is at its peak.

There is no source of shade, no source of water – no solace from the heat. Just hot scorching sand and fire-blazing heat from the Sun above.

What are you burning with? Is it desire? Passion? Frustration? Nobody said that entering the desert was going to be easy.

Sit and think about your expectations, own them. Did you have any?

The desert is a metaphor for life. One doesn't just simply walk out of the desert. It is a process to intentionally enter the desert and it is a tough process to maneuver through life as a desert.

There are times in your life where you will be thirsty, parched and desperate. There are times in your life where you are going to be hot, overwhelmed and perspiring with frustration or aggravation.

Who will quench your thirst? Who will provide you shade. Who is your support team? Who do you reach out to?

When one embraces desert sage witchcraft as solitary or pack tradition, it is vital to be consciously aware of the ebb and flow.

We each have different landscapes and no two deserts look the same. So we must be gentle with the journey. Some days there will be plenty of animal messengers, maybe even too many. Other days, there will not be any.

You may have to journey into your meditative desert and really ask for direction. Just know that the struggle is real and shift perspective. Is it really a struggle or just an off day?

For me, having a daily devotion and way of greeting each animal, plant and person sets the tone for my entire day and helps enhance the relationships that I forge along the way.

Be ever mindful that each step I take is on sacred ground, for each step taken is made upon the great Mother. But again, some days are better than others. "Just like Mama Moon – we go in phases."

Be gentle and enjoy the process of living a more animistic life.

WHY A WOLF PACK AND NOT A COVEN?

This is a loaded question! I personally know many practitioners within the Craft and each one has a different coven story; very rarely are they good.

I myself have been a member of four covens and, after six years of leading my own coven, I determined that coven work sucks. It's hard! The one who leads is always on the chopping block, no matter how much time and energy they invest into their coven members.

The hierarchy within a coven is not appreciated. Some leaders deserve that lack of appreciation and others do not.

My best advice before joining a coven is to do research, ask questions and first observe the coven in action, if possible. Get to know some of the members and, most importantly, read their sacred agreements. What makes their coven tick?

My best advice before starting a coven is: know your shit. Be prepared to be questioned on everything and be humble. Leading a coven is not a glorified position; it's like being a priest or priestess – it is an act of service. It takes time, an exhausting amount of time! The leader is always first to arrive and last to leave, bearing the brunt of all the work with little if any appreciation; most often criticism.

Have an agenda for your coven – what tradition are you honoring and why? Most importantly, and the most difficult thing is to create sacred agreements and make sure everyone, including yourself, is honoring them.

Coven work is great, don't get me wrong. I would much rather do group magick than solitary. The energy raised with a group of like-minded individuals is pure bliss. Celebrating the Wheel of the Year is ideal with community, with family, and that is what a coven should strive to be. Feasting following one of the sabbat ceremonies is my most favorite thing.

For a while, I led a grove (thirteen or more witches), which, technically, I still do. However, instead of having an acting high priest and high priestesses leading all the Wheel of the Year sabbats, we have shifted our focus to wolf pack energy and my lover of twenty-one years is my magical partner.

Together, he and I serve our pack as Lord and Lady of our land; Mama Wolf and Papa Bear. We honor each individual that circles with us a space to be themselves and we celebrate that. We welcome the fact that our pack is full of a variety of wild ones that each vibrate with their own unique, authentic pizzazz.

Wolf pack modality reinforces unity without the religious stereotypes of a 'commune' or 'congregation' – we welcome all who circle with us with a place in our pack. They do not need to prove their worth; they just need to show up, participate fully and understand that "the strength of the pack is the wolf, and the strength of the wolf is the pack."

Since we have shifted from a grove to a wolf pack, our numbers have increased. We are seeing more families join us for our Wheel of the Year sabbats than ever before. We have also added a geo-climbing dome for the small children and have made it their 'kinder dome' or 'pup den'. This is a space for them to gather, play and celebrate their own magick.

Wolves are incredible animals who are deeply devoted to their pack. They are the poster image of what an ideal family can be when everyone works together for the greater good – and that is each other's survival. Every wolf within the pack knows its place and role within the structure of the pack.

Their hierarchy, in years past, was greatly misunderstood, as society once believed wolves were extremely aggressive and detrimental to the planet because they were seen as fierce predators who kill anyone and everything.

Not to mention that wolves have been linked to witchcraft for a very, very long time. Their hierarchy is really no different than the one that exists within your own home and extended family. The only difference is that we no longer live in tribes, like our ancestors did.

Our elders; aunts, uncles, cousins, siblings, nieces, nephews, children and grandchildren, all live in their own homes far away from each other. Very rarely does a family get together for a reunion more than once every other year.

We, as a society, have lost touch with what really matters, and that is the devotion to family and pack. We don't treat each other as pack mates – we treat each other as competitors, strangers and often we look at other people as insignificant.

What I love about shifting from coven/grove to wolf pack is that everyone who circles with us feels like family. We are deeply invested in each other's individual and family survival, rather than just a casual hello and hug following a high holy Wheel of the Year sabbat – we engage with each other.

Our pups (children) play with each other, we help each other move, go to each other's homes for dinner and when one of our wolves within our pack is not feeling well – we all lend a paw.

In the book, *The Wisdom of Wolves: Lessons from the Sawtooth Pack*, the authors Jim & Jamie Dutcher express that "The more we know about wolves, the more we know about ourselves, and the more we can pass on to our children."

Wolves are the spiritual embodiment of America's lost connection with Nature. They are social. They need each other. They communicate, cooperate, teach their young, and share the duties of day to day life. A wolf knows who it is as an individual and wolves see their pack mates as individuals. They are emotionally intelligent and care about what happens to themselves, family members and friends. Each wolf has within it a concept of how its actions are perceived by others. They are capable of empathy, compassion, apology and encouragement.

This is what society needs! We need to start seeing everyone as one of the pack. We need to take care of our elders, making sure they are seated first, fed first and checked on, more than just occasionally.

We need to look to the pups (children) for reminders of how to live a more conscious life. Children see the world with excitement! My granddaughter has taught me more about magick and living mindfully than anyone or anything else. Children are the answer. They are the greatest teachers.

When we take the time to really teach children about the earth, plants, insects and animals, they are open-minded, unlike adults – who are set in their ways. Just yesterday, while working in the garden, my granddaughter and I moved some logs and discovered a network of earthworms. We sat down and connect with the worms. We had conversations and even picked up a worm for her to see how transparent they are and then we kindly placed it back into the dirt and watched as it wriggled down into the earth.

When we sit and engage with each other, even if we are just passing in the grocery store, those few moments can shift one's entire day! We currently are living in a state of the unknown – fear, and things feel very unsafe.

We are muted, tethered and confined. As humans, we are adaptable and can shift things for the greater good, but we have to start somewhere. Why can't it be with a simple act of kindness?

Wolves are extraordinary mirrors of how we, as humans, can live more ecologically, efficiently and experience more happiness and connection with each other and the land.

Wolves have helper animals along the way such as bear and raven. Ravens have been known to be nannies to wolf pups. They frequently visit the den, cleaning it up, playing with the wolves and interacting with them – they communicate. It is said that if you want to know where wolves are in the wilderness – look up and ask the ravens to show you. Ravens will lead wolves to their dinner. They are the messengers.

Wolves will tear open the flesh of the carcass that the ravens have found and, together, they will feast. Bears are not too far behind as they are keenly aware of the wolves and ravens relationship and they too benefit.

Bears will scavenge the remaining carcass. While bears and wolves are predators and have been known to attack and kill each other – they do have a special relationship.

In 2013, Finnish photographer, Lassi Rautiainen, observed a remarkable friendship between a female grey wolf and a male brown bear. The two were filmed and photographed for ten consecutive days interacting with each other, hunting together, playing and sharing their meals.

What a gift to witness such a beautiful and unexpected relationship. Whenever I see the pictures surface on social media I always tag my lover as his primary spirit animal is a brown bear and mine is a grey wolf. For me, this relationship mirrors hope; a hope that, as humans, despite our differences, we can come together. We can get along, play together, work together and sit down at the end of the day and share a feast.

Instead of spoon-feeding people dogma, what if we allowed individuals to show up as who they are, as they really are, and just practiced acceptance? We don't have to always think, feel or believe in the same things. While sharing commonalities opens the door for communication and being able to relate to each other, it really isn't neccessary is it?

There is a closed, exclusion that occurs within a coven that creates tension, hurt feelings and resentment. While covens are primarily focused on teaching a particular tradition or branch, they lack the friendship and camaraderie that Hollywood portrays.

Instead, most covens only meet up for workshops and sabbat ceremonies. They very rarely interact with each other outside of these set meeting times. Switching from coven/grove to wolf pack has opened up so many doors and has allowed so many individuals to feel safe, accepted and celebrated for their individuality – not just at events, workshops and high holy sabbat celebrations – but every day.

INCORPORATING ANIMISM INTO OUR DIALOGUE

When moving into desert sage witchcraft and living a more animistic approach to one's solitary or pack magick, the words one speaks create one's experience. After all, to create a magick spell, one needs to speak their intent out loud or literally spell it out.

The Universe is amazing and will gift us exactly what we ask for, we just need to be more specific. 'Abracadabra' is an Aramaic word which means: "What I speak is what I create."

If you want to start seeing the people in your life as animals and open the doorway to increased love and compassion, the words you speak to describe each other really do create the relationship. We live in a world that already does this; we just don't always put the two together.

We are constantly referring to each other as animals in a negative sense, or maybe somewhat comical, and sometimes complimentary. You have probably heard some if not all of the idioms (common phrases which mean something different from their literal meaning but can be understood because of their popular use) used below:

- Let the cat out of the bag.
- In hog heaven.
- Cat got your tongue?
- Butterflies in your stomach?
- Memory like an elephant.
- Thick like an ox.

In our wolf pack we have started to incorporate more animal references when we talk to each other. Such as: lend a paw, time to show teeth and time to bite, let us howl in celebration, circle up, sniff it out before reacting, trust your paws...

The ideal being to remember that we are all animals and when we can relate to each other as animals, it lessens our desire to step into ego/human brain and judge each other.

As wolf, I know that I am territorial in a protective manner. With my lover, he is both strong like a bear and stubborn. My daughter is a lion and she will roar if her lounging time is interrupted. We are again using animal terms to refer to each other all the time! We use Nature idioms as well such as:

- Ray of sunshine – Drop in the ocean.
- Can't see the forest for the trees – Down to earth.
- Making a mountain out of a mole hill – Go with the flow.

Being conscious about the words we speak is magic! The power behind the words we choose to express is profound and each word spoken shapes our reality. One simple word spoken out of context or with little intention can create damage.

As witches, activists and animists, we need to be more aware of what the words we are speaking are creating. Part of walking the Wheel of the Year with animals as our guides is to learn from them; to observe them and to communicate with them.

Have you ever yelled at an animal and saw it immediately respond with fear and crouching? We yell at other humans all the time with little regard to how they may feel. Yet, when we yell at our dog and they give us that look of sorrow and fear, we immediately feel horrible! Why are we not feeling horrible when we yell at each other as people?

Start taking notice of how you engage with yourself, your pack and those in your surrounding community. Step into a more conscious way of living. One thing that may help, if you already have a coven/grove or pack, is to take everyone through the 'connecting with your primary spirit animal meditation,' found in Chapter Two. This activating will help you and everyone else begin to see each other as animals rather than strangers.

HONORING ONE'S LANDSCAPE AND ANIMAL TEACHERS

This is the core practice of desert sage witchcraft. When an individual takes the time to get to know the animals and landscape they live with then their gateway to establishing a more conscious way of life begins. The individual enters a state of eating, sleeping and breathing their practice.

While there are sabbat ceremonies and animals to take notice of within this book, starting a journal is a great way to increase connection with one's world. Spend time each day outside and step into observation mode. What time of day is it? What season are you currently experiencing? What animals are active this time of day and year? For example, in my desert landscape there are certain plants and animals that are prevalent at certain times of year; these indicate which season and energy is most dominant.

The main mission of this tradition is to allow one a practice that is centered on the individual and the land one lives in. It is very hard for me as a desert wolf to connect with the ocean landscape and animals – just like it is difficult for one who lives near the ocean to connect with the desert.

Taking time to anchor into our personal surroundings, plants and animals will only deepen our solitary and pack practice.

As one who frequently travels, I know that I can take the desert magick with me but there is a more profound magickal connection when I allow myself to be open and taught by my current surroundings. When I travel, the first thing I do upon arrival is get my bearings. I connect with the land itself, then observe. What animals do I see? Which plants? What are the elements expressing to me?

THE MAGICK IS IN THE MOMENT

In the movie *Kung Fu Panda* (another animistic movie), 'Po' the Panda has a conversation with 'Master Oogway' the wise turtle, who offers this sage advice (which actually comes from Eleanor Roosevelt): "Yesterday is history. Tomorrow is a mystery. But today is a gift. That is why it's called the present."

There are many ways to train oneself to be more mindfully present. We can slow down and remember to breathe like the manatee. We can cuddle up with our pack and share stories of things that make us grateful. We can even go outside and lay upon the earth, connect heart to heart with the mama.

Being a witch is being mindful of one's personal connection and relationship with one's surrounding landscape, plant allies, insects and animals. To live a more magical life, one simply needs to just put down the phone, walk away from the computer and go outside. There is a whole world out there filled with medicine and magick – we just have to start opening our eyes and paying attention.

DEVOTION THROUGH PRAYER

What is prayer? Well, by definition it is: "A request for help or expression of thanks addressed to a god, goddess, higher power or the divine, as the individual defines it."

Growing up in a Mormon home, we had a checklist for prayer. In other words, children were taught an opening, middle and closing. The prayers were very much scripted in design and, for me, lacked connection. I never felt that God was listening.

When I pray, it is a very personal conversation with the divine as I define it. Sometimes I pray to a god, goddess, animal or plant ally. The difference is that, on a personal level, there is no worship. The gods, goddesses and higher power or divine already exist within me – when I pray to them, it is more to activate their attributes as a mirror allowing me to see those attributes within myself.

In each Wheel of the Year sabbat ceremony, there are prayers, or rather invocations, to the animals being honored. In the tradition of desert sage witchcraft, it is helpful to set up an altar that is dedicated to one's path of embracing animism and place in the center an image or statue of one's PSA (primary spirit animal).

Each day, go to your altar and connect with your PSA through prayer and daily devotion. One prayer that I do often in front of my wolf altar is: "Oh Great Wolf, help my paws to move me in a direction that will increase awareness and good health within myself. Help me to walk low to the ground, that I may be more connected with source and better serve my pack as a bridge and conduit of your devotion."

Praying is an act of devotion and there is no right or wrong way.

Speak and create. Abracadabra!

FREQUENTLY ASKED QUESTIONS

- What is the difference between a totem animal and primary spirit animal?

The difference is that a 'totem' serves as an emblem that best represents a group, clan or tribe. That totem is their main animal. Totems can also be plants, or objects. Here at the Utah Goddess Temple, our totem animal is the wolf.

One's primary spirit animal is one's personal soul reflection of an animal. These can be mirrors of the individual. There are days where I connect with other animals in meditation or in person. All are considered teachers and messengers, whether they are in the flesh or in spirit form.

- Can a person receive more than one animal in the connection meditation?

Absolutely! Oftentimes, this is because of a shift or point of unsettled transition in the person's life where numerous animals volunteer to come forward as reminders and mirrors of the individual's strength.

Another reason multiple animals can come through is that they may be primary spirit animals from previous periods in one's life. Years ago I connected with owl for about eight years. When owl shows up in my meditations, I know that I am to harness that power of owl and do some much needed research.

Journaling is an excellent tool and once you sit down and connect with the meditation and all that comes through it by writing it down, you have a new perspective to digest and observe. So, following meditations – write things down. Then trust that the reason why multiple animals come through will appear while you release onto the paper.

BONUS MEDITATIONS TO ASSIST YOU IN CONNECTING WITH ANIMALS AS MESSENGERS

Animals as Sacred Messenger Meditation

Sitting or lying in a comfortable position, begin to bring your focus to your breath.

Taking a nice deep inhale followed by a deep cleansing exhale. Continue this pattern of inhale and exhale until you begin to feel your entire physical body relax from head to toe.

Then bring your awareness to your mind, letting go of worries, stresses and anything distracting.

Inhale…2….3…4…and exhale…2…3…4…

(repeat three times)

With your physical body relaxed, you are now ready to journey deeper into your subconscious mind. See in your mind's eye that you are sitting or lying down in a safe space outdoors somewhere in Nature. Feel as a circle of stones begins to push up from the ground creating a circle around you.

The stones will appear in whatever shape or form they desire, the key is to simply allow them to contain you, safe guarding you from the mundane realm.

With the stones around you, there is a calm sensation of containment that begins to caress you.

In this circle of stones, you can't help but feel safe, held and anchored to Nature.

Give yourself permission to move around this inner circle of stones.

Observing how there are archways at each quarter direction.

One at the gateway of the east, south, west and north.

Feel as you walk around, making a full circle inside, where you return to sit on the center stone – a large flat slab that has appeared where you first sat or were lying down.

Allow yourself to settle in on this center stone. Connect with earth upon earth.

Bring your awareness back to your breath and clear your mind.

This is a connection stone – you have come here for a specific intent and purpose.

Allow yourself to activate that. With your palms open, in the pose of reception, call upon an animal messenger to join you here in this circle of stones.

(pause)

Observe how the animal enters through one of the directional gateways and sits upon the stone slab with you, here in the center. The key to activating animal energy is through observation, not manipulation or elements of control. So, allow the animal to move in its own way, at its own pace. Simply watch. Simply allow.

With the animal inside your inner circle – it has chosen to respond to your seeking, to your intent and your purpose. The animal here is your teacher, your mentor, your messenger.

Lower your gaze and open your mind, your ears and your senses to its guidance.

(pause)

Once you have received, offer gratitude in exchange. See the animal leave your inner circle sanctuary through whichever gateway it chooses and begin to breathe your awareness back to the present.

See the standing stones lower back into the ground and feel yourself once more in your present state. Feeling whole, balanced and appreciative.

- Journal your experience.

ANIMAL PREDATOR AND PREY MIRROR MEDITATION

Sitting in a nice comfortable position, close your eyes we begin with your breath.

Take in a nice deep cleansing inhale…and exhale it out… breathe in… and breathe out…

Now breathe in…2…3…4… and breathe out…2…3…4…

(repeat 3 times)

Now breathing at your own pace, allow yourself to just relax and let go with each exhale.

As you breathe, you feel your entire body sink into a very comfortable, safe state of relaxation.

Now that you are relaxed, I want you to simply use your imagination and see yourself sitting in the middle of a meadow. It is a bright sunny day and you can feel the warmth of the Sun on your face.

You feel the soft gentle breeze on your skin as you sit here in the most beautiful meadow you have ever seen. Really see the wildflowers swaying, feel the grass underneath you and, looking out, you see the edge of the meadow surrounded by tall oak and aspen trees – framing this sacred space.

Sitting here observing Nature, you begin to hear movement from the forest; you may see a shadow moving through the trees. Observe as your spirit animal steps out into the meadow and moves towards you. Your spirit animal has a message for you today so its movement is strong and precise.

Watch as your spirit animal joins you in the middle of the meadow. Sitting here with your spirit animal right in front of you, inches from your face – your eyes lock and you gaze into each other's soul for a brief moment. Spend a few moments connecting with your spirit animal, reach out and make physical contact, feel the power of your spirit animal as you touch it, feel its strength, remember that your animal chose you and that you are safe. Spend some time reconnecting. We have invited your spirit animal into the meadow today to do some shadow work and to remember that we are both predator and prey. I want you to ask your spirit animal to show you what it's like for your spirit animal to be predator. How does it move when it goes into predator mode, does it sniff out the area, dig into the earth, do the hairs on its back raise?

Watch your spirit animal demonstrate predator attack mode. How do you physically feel while you observe the predator? Now ask your spirit animal to show you what being prey feels and looks like.

Can you feel the heart racing? Can you feel the fear and the need to run?

Tell your spirit animal "thank you for the demonstration," and now just sit and hold your spirit animal.

Reestablish trust and respect. It is a very vulnerable experience to show someone your prey and predator characteristics. So, really spend some time physically connecting with your spirit animal.

Our spirit animal is us in our most natural, primal, animal state. Observing your spirit animal as both predator and prey is like looking into a mirror and seeing how you respond when you are being attacked or how you do the attacking. This can be a very emotional experience and a very eye opening one.

Allow yourself the opportunity to accept that we are both predator and prey in our lives, every day.

When you are ready, see yourself standing up with your spirit animal by your side as you both leave the meadow. Feel your fingers begin to move your feet beginning to move as you slowly come back to the present – feeling both humbled and aware. When you are ready, open your eyes.

- Journal your experience.

RIGHT NOW IN YOUR LIFE, HOW HAVE YOU ALLOWED YOURSELF TO BECOME VICTIM TO ANOTHER?

Choosing to be offended, taking things personally, reacting.

RIGHT NOW IN YOUR LIFE, HOW HAVE YOU ALLOWED YOURSELF TO BECOME PREDATOR TO ANOTHER?

Being jealous, coveting another's life, gossiping.

HOW DO YOU FIND BALANCE?

Stop caring about what others think, say or do – live your life authentically. Don't compare or compromise yourself – recognize and embrace that there is both a time and a place to be both predator and prey, and that's OK.

MAKE A LIST OF YOUR PREDATOR AND PREY CHARACTERISTICS

Predator:	Prey:
1.	1.
2.	2.
3.	3.
4.	4.
5.	5.

EMBRACING YOUR SHADOW SELF OR MANEUVERING YOUR INNER DESERT

Please consider that the things you perceive as faults, negative patterns or things you do not like about yourself, are actually your assets. In other words, your weaknesses become your strengths.

"It's your life purpose to shine light on the hardened and petrified parts of you. To spread your light on Earth, first and foremost reach out to the darkness within."

In other words, one does not need to focus on what needs to be remedied in the world, but instead, on what needs to be healed within.

Once you embrace your own journey, your light will shine out and inspire others to do the same.

Your Perceived Faults:	Your Perceived Truths:
1.	1.
2.	2.
3.	3.
4.	4.
5.	5.

This is a great eye-opening exercise to do with a partner, spouse or within a coven or wolf pack; giving everyone space to sit and really see that their predator and prey aspects do not always match up with others and that they are not always negative.

The hardest part is to make these lists from a mindful state where they are expressed without judgment.

THE HONEST TRUTH

While embracing a more conscious animistic way of life creates overall balance, it has its struggles. For example, in relationships it's not always easy to just dismiss the behavior of someone based solely off what their primary spirit animal is. Individuals still need to be accountable for their behavior, words and engagements with others.

Ultimately, as individuals, we can only be responsible for ourselves and our reactions. Some things are not forgivable or forgettable. Sometimes, no matter how open minded you are and how much you want to believe in someone else, there are times where the bear and the wolf will need to go their separate ways. Some animals are just more solitary than others. There is a time to nip at the heels and there is a time to admit defeat and retreat back into one's den.

Our predator and prey aspects may not be liked or appreciated by those we are in relationships with. Is communication a tool that would be beneficial? Can two people sit down and really discuss their differences without exerting opinions, judgments, expectations and obligations? Someday I hope we, the human species, as a society, can do just that.

For me, working with animals instead of deities has strengthened my connection to my landscape and the animals that actually live in my landscape. Animism isn't just animals! I can see the animals; observe them at their peak time of year and day. I can see them as mirrors. No matter where you live, you will have animals nearby that you can connect with.

In the morning, take note of which animals, insects and birds are most active. Do this for the afternoon and evening too. Then start taking note of the seasons and which animals are mating, birthing and preparing. This simple technique of observing will help you develop a full calendar year of animal guides.

My life would feel very hollow without the animals in it. My home would most certainly be empty. Animals have and are a magick all to themselves. Whilst in my garden, I love to just sit and watch, then wait with anticipation to see who will come and visit.

In the spring, that first robin is such a breath of fresh air and lets me know it's almost time to plant. In the summer, the buzz of the bumble bees reminds me that there is much work to be done and the Sun has allowed for more time to accomplish the tasks at hand. In the fall, when the squirrels are busy gathering and prepping, it reminds me that it's time to take advantage of the garden goodies and preserve and store as much as I can for winter. Then, when that first snow falls and the earth is tucked under that thick blanket of white and the songbirds come out a bit later in the day to sit in the Sun, I am reminded to move slower, spend as much time as possible doing things that bring me warmth.

The animals move us through the seasons, they are such a natural part of the order of things that we often take them for granted. They really do show us how to live in harmony with each other and with the land.

Our ancestors spent much time learning as students of the land and the animals. If we could just turn off our phones, unplug the television and go outside, maybe we could see there is a different way to live amongst each other and still remain authentic individuals. Maybe we could see that we can coexist?

BONUS CHAPTER

An Anthology of Animal Mirrors

By now, you are more aware that animals speak to us through many different facets each and every day.

We see them in the Tarot, when we go outside, in books, in meditation and just about every waking day we will see an animal or insect of some kind. What are they saying to us? What are they showing us as mirrors? Can we take the time to absorb their attributes as sources of inspiration?

Ant: hardworking, devoted, perseverance, loyal
Alligator: mysterious, elusive, thick skinned, powerful
Armadillo: protected, smart, resourceful
Angelfish: beauty, exotic

Badger: productive, boundaries
Bat: shadow, intuitive, nocturnal
Barn owl: wise, knowledge, intelligence
Bear: mother, confident, protector
Bearded dragon: proud, agile, guarded
Beaver: prepared, swift, resourceful
Beetle: layered, tough
Bengal tiger: piercing, grounded
Birds: perspective, majestic
Bighorn sheep: sharp, agile, domestic, wise
Butterfly: celebration, joy, beauty

Camel: patient, survivor
Cat: affectionate, royal, mischievous
Chameleon: ability to blend into any situation, cautious, patient, mindful
Cheetah: quick, agile, solitary

Chicken: ancient, provider, protective
Chimpanzee: empathetic, intelligent
Cicada: sing, ancient, messenger
Cougar: pounce, proactive, fierce
Crab: guarded, trickster
Crane: grace
Chipmunk: prepared, quick
Cow: fertile, mother, nourisher
Cockroach: unbeatable, survivor
Coyote: playful, unpredictable, talkative
Crocodile: silent, watcher, strong

Dog: loyal, obedient, trustworthy
Dolphin: knowledge, smart
Deer: instincts, gentle, trust
Desert tortoise: ancient wisdom, teacher
Dragonfly: peaceful, joy, transformation

Eagle: noble, protector, symbol of the Sun
Electric eel: stimulating, defensive, exotic
Elephant: strong, proud, ancient mother
Elk: teacher, guardian of pathways
Emu: solid, quick, guardian

AN ANTHOLOGY OF ANIMAL MIRROR

Falcon: keen sight, new perspective
Ferret: mischievous, creative, gatherer
Fox: playful, sneaky
Fish: abundance
Frog: adaptable

Giant panda: balanced
Giraffe: awkward, able to reach higher
Goat: steady, durable
Gorilla: comfort, strength
Gecko: surprising
Grasshopper: hungry
Goose: protective
Gopher: relentless

Horse: helpful, supportive, steady
Hare: inclusive
Hummingbird: joyful
Hyena: unrestrained, joyful
Humpback whale: gentle, musical, communicative

Iguana: intimidating

Jaguar: holds space, secretive, fierce
Jellyfish: mesmerizing, defensive
Jackal: playful, mischievous, sneaky

King cobra: royal, noble, warning
Koala: cuddly
Kangaroo: deceptive
Kiwi: unusual, rare
Komodo dragon: defender

Leopard: camouflage, elusive
Llama: confidant
Lion: calm, strength, power
Ladybug: predator, good omen
Lemur: matriarchal, resilient
Lizard: adaptable, rebirth, confidence
Lobster: responsive, muscular, protective
Lynx: mysterious, mischievous, playful

Mole: depth, dedicated, instinctual
Monkey: playful, intelligent, willing to learn
Macaw: colorful, communication
Meerkat: cautious, playful, pack-oriented
Moose: magnificent, gentle, massive
Moth: dance, shadow, peaceful
Mourning dove: love, graceful
Mule: travel, companionship, loyal
Mouse: sneaky, quiet, observer

Newt: rejuvenation, sleek
Narwhal: magic, mysterious, majestic
Nightingale: healing, musical

Ocelot: curious, playful, agile
Orangutan: laughter, playful, curious, problem-solver
Octopus: misunderstood, helper, flexible
Ostrich: fearful, cautious, confident
Oyster: hidden beauty, transformation
Opossum: survival, docile, unpredictable
Otter: playful, family-oriented, loving

Pangolin: shy, endangered, gatekeeper
Peacock: arrogant, mesmerizing, narcissism
Panther: elusive, mysterious, quick
Pelican: calm, glide, perspective
Pig: joy, content, intelligent
Piranha: deadly, vicious, defender
Platypus: unique, deadly defense
Puma: fierce, elusive
Parrot: communication, intelligence, adaptability
Pigeon: resilient, persistent, determined to survive
Pheasant: smart, aggressive
Polar bear: camouflage, protector
Puffin: swimmers, curious, loyal

AN ANTHOLOGY OF ANIMAL MIRRORS

Quail: communication, stunning, family oriented

Rabbit: speed, agility, fertility
Rat: resilient, persistent, determined to survive
Red panda: rare, evolved, resourceful
Raccoon: resourceful, intelligent
Rattlesnake: boundaries, warning omen, rebirth can be painful
Reindeer: fertility, motherhood, transformation
Robin: messenger of spring
Rhinoceros: stubborn, prideful, protective, noble

Scorpion fish: exotic, defender
Sea lion: strong, thick-skinned
Seahorse: transitional, mysterious
Snake: rebirthing, transformational
Snow leopard: elusive, mysterious, rare
Snowy owl: camouflage, magic, mystery
Spade foot toad: resilient
Squid: unique, adaptable, big-hearted
Salamander: diverse, smooth, nocturnal
Sea turtle: ancient, ancestor, protective
Sheep: gentle, obedient, follower
Sea sponge: absorb, recycle, transformation
Sea star: elegant, mysterious
Sugar glider: agile, nocturnal, flight
Salmon: steadfast, dedicated, ancestral magick
Scorpion: mysterious, truth can sting
Shark: fierce, powerful, dynamic
Sand dollar: magical, social, peaceful

Skunk: mischievous, curious, headstrong
Sloth: methodical, strong, slow
Snail: spiral energy, asymmetry, charismatic

Termite: ravenous, recyclers, aerators
Toucan: colorful, attractive, communication
Turkey: magic feathers, large, domesticated
Tiger shark: tropical, dramatic, hunters

Umbrella bird: powerful, unique

Vampire bat: mysterious, occult
Vulture: watchful, patient, devouring, scavenger

Water buffalo: strong, noble, steadfast
Weasel: sneaky, quick, surefooted
Wolverine: aggressor, warrior, fierce
Woodpecker: messenger, alert, beware
Wombat: docile, strong, resourceful
Wolf spider: mother, hunter, defender
Woolly mammoth: massive, ambitious
Walrus: social, thick-skinned, intelligent, kind
Wasp: predator, creators, ingenious
Wolf: leader, loyal, service oriented

Yak: trusted, resourceful, resilient

Zebra: balance, unique, communicative

In my heart of hearts I firmly believe that all humans are capable of living an animistic life. Everyone on this planet can and should start looking to the animals, plants and seasons as guides of how to step in and be more consciously aware and more importantly mindful.

We have within us the responsibility to care for and protect this planet. For we need this planet! Our children's, children need this planet. Small acts can and do shape the reality in which we live. By teaching one child to love, honor and respect all living things, they become a mirror to others. We have to start somewhere. Why not start within?

What is your connection with animals? When did you learn to overpower them or to be taught by them? My childhood was a blessing and all the animals that came into our home were family, not pets. They listened, loved and gave 100% of themselves. Why can't we, as humans, do that? Why can't we see other humans as just another animal or just another species of animals? Why can't we honor the individual and still offer love, respect and devotion? Would it change anything?

Each day I have on this planet is a gift. Each animal that I come into contact with, whether physically or energetically, is a teacher, mentor, messenger and guide. Each plant that I grow, consume and digest for nourishment is my medicine. Each person I meet along the way is another member of the pack.

We all eat, sleep and breathe on this great sphere we call the Mama. How about we do it with more dignity, respect and take the responsibility of being stewards, light-workers, healers, witches, Pagans and animists seriously?

The children are watching us. The animals are watching us. Let's not destroy their future with our arrogance, ignorance and egos.

Let's stop the madness by being the change.
With love.

– Lady Wolf

About the Author & Artist

Lady Wolf is a triple ordained Wiccan high priestess honoring the Dianic, Alexandrian/Hermetic and eclectic lineages. She is a Reiki Master, licensed crystal therapist, Cacao Priestess, animist witch, shapeshifting guide, spirit animal conduit, master herbalist, green witch, Mother & Priestess of the Utah Goddess Temple (Utah's FIRST dedicated Pagan temple), ceremonial priestess, mother of three, grandmother, lover, oracular, minister, daughter of Brigid, daughter of Odin and is a wild wolf woman.

For the past twenty-six years, Lady Wolf has been actively birthing her witchcraft tradition; 'desert sage witchcraft,' which is deeply devoted to High Desert magick and animals as guides.

To contact Lady Wolf for public speaking engagements please email: desertsagewitchcraft@gmail.com
You can follow her on Instagram: @utahgoddess or **Facebook:** @utahgoddesstemple and @ladywolfauthor